Prayers That Are Different

†

PRAYERS
That Are Different

by

Frederick W. Lewis

William B. Eerdmans Publishing Company
Grand Rapids, Michigan

Printed in the United States of America
Library of Congress catalog card number 64-16583

In beloved memory
of
GRACE HOWELL LEWIS

Foreword

The plan of this book, as far as I know, is unique. This divergence from other books of prayers appears in the following ways:

1. It is not a collection of prayers from various centuries, countries and viewpoints, but from one writer who endeavors to voice the approach of the average worshipper in the American churches of today.
2. The prayers are not of a general or comprehensive nature, but devoted to single topics.
3. The book is not limited to one prayer for each topic, but in many cases provides from two to four prayers.
4. It deals not only with the special days of the ecclesiastical year, but also with many other public days or seasons, i.e., Commencement, Autumn, etc.

If these prayers make any more vivid the living presence of God, and if they cause any more thorough commitment to Jesus Christ, and if they promote any larger fruits of the Spirit, and if they bring a redeeming message to any wayward souls, and hasten the day when every knee shall bow to our Lord, in any one of these instances I shall have the satisfaction of knowing that this book has fulfilled its mission.

FREDERICK W. LEWIS

Contents

PART ONE

Themes Related to Home, Church, Nation, and School

PART TWO

Miscellaneous Religious Themes

Title	*Page*
Our Brother's Keeper	142
Our Girls	143
Our Sure Refuge	144
Paradise	144
Patience	145
The Peace of Sunday Morning	146
The Perfect Man	146
Pioneers in Space	147
The Players' Prayer	148
Poverty	148
Power	149
Principles	150
Protection	150
Religion Beyond the Pale	151
Religion Is Second Nature	152
Repentance	152
Responsiveness to the Unseen	153
Salvation	154
Self-Surveys	154
Sheep or Goats	155
The Sick	156
Sincerity	156
Sorrow	157
The Strain of City Life	157
Suffering	158
Supreme Loyalty	159
Sympathy	160
Temperance	160
They that Mourn	161
They that Suffer	162
Unconscious Influence	162
Unfaltering Trust	163
Unused Talents	164
Uphill	164
Vanity	165
Worthy Football	166

Part I

Themes Related to
Home, Church, Nation and School

HOLY ADVENT

Make ye ready the way of the Lord, . . . And all flesh shall see the salvation of God
—Luke 3:4, 6

Lord Jesus, as the time draws near to celebrate Thy coming to save mankind and provide in Thyself the image of God, we would hail the sacred joys of this season. Thou wast the Rose of Sharon brightly blooming 'mid the wastes of human wickedness. Thou wast "the Bright and Morning Star" of glory, yea, "the Light of the World" heralded by angels in sparkling white above Bethlehem's plain. When "the whole world was lost in the darkness of sin" Thou didst not decline the role of Saviour because of our humble place in God's starry universe, but Thou didst come to conduct this wandering planet back into its orbit among the heavenly host. O Thou peerless Son of David, Thou art David's Greater Son; for edifying as were the Psalms of the ancient singer, yet no man ever spoke like Thee. Thy words were electric with power and light. Praise God that this is life eternal: to know God as the heavenly Father and Thee as Saviour, and God's other Self. All hail to the issues of Bethlehem, Nazareth, Jerusalem and Calvary! Amen.

THE TIME DRAWS NEAR

Let us now go even unto Bethlehem, and see this thing that is come to pass —Luke 2:15

O God, Father of our Lord Jesus Christ, we thank Thee that the prophets knew in advance of the Messianic coming, who by faith were well pleasing unto God and endured as seeing Him who is invisible. And now, as Bethlehem draws near, help us to realize how it is the realization of burning hopes which made servants of God heroic for two millenniums preceding the Advent and how, since His coming, He has been a Pillar of Cloud and Fire for advancing civilization, and the glorious Saviour of a host of redeemed men and women. May all of us be found in the group expecting the Divine Child. Let Christmas carols roll over the earth proclaiming "Everywhere, everywhere Christmas to-night." Let the morning stars sing together. Let everything in heaven and earth take up the shout, "Hosanna to the son of David: Blessed is he that cometh in the name of the Lord; Hosanna in the highest." Amen.

AUTUMN

I love Thee, O Jehovah, my strength,
Jehovah is my rock, and my fortress, and my deliverer;
My God, my rock, in whom I will take refuge
—Psalm 18:1

O Thou ever-self-revealing God, who dost speak to us in many languages other than words, we thank Thee for the eternal message of Nature. We bless Thee for the rhythm of the seasons that bring us the virgin graces of spring and the sacrament of summer. And now we are grateful for the delights and duties and lessons that come to us in the mellow days of the turning leaves. "Day unto day uttereth speech." As thou dost paint these fleeting pictures of flaming crimson and gold upon canvasses of maple and oak, may we catch the cheer Thou would'st impart as inspiring memories, to treasure up against the sterner days of winter yet to come. Yea, Lord, our hearts leap up to a nobler truth. They spring with a hope yet more joyous and of farther reach. The autumnal pageant assures to our believing souls the sight of eternal things passing the fairest of the glories of earth. O Lord, evermore sustain us by this immortal hope. In the Name of Nature's God. Amen.

AUTUMN

My flesh and my heart faileth; but God is the strength of my heart and my portion for ever.
—Psalm 73:26

O God, as the seasons come and go and Autumn is here, a peace which passeth understanding possesseth all Thy creatures. All sounds and scenes are blended into a still and lovely harmony. We are pleased, heavenly Father, to believe that October is one more evidence of Thy infinite tenderness. How gradually dost Thou break to the year the news that it is growing old! In Autumn's pageant August's goldenrod is still flaming when the aster hangs out its purple banners. The past and the future overlap their colors and the symbols of both memory and hope are interblended. So, O Lord, if there comes to every man a day in which he knows he is growing old, Thou dost temper the thought by reminders of mellow fruitfulness and by tokens of approaching glory, so that sweetly and insensibly he traverses Autumn's road, knowing that, as the falling leaf is enfolded again in the bosom of Mother Earth, so "the spirit shall return to God who gave it." Amen.

AUTUMN

The leaf fadeth from off the vine, and . . . the fading leaf from the fig-tree –Isaiah 34:4

There is a temptation, O Lord, to feel that "the melancholy days have come, the saddest of the year," for with the songs of summer fled and with the long, gloomy winter ahead, with the merry birds winging to the South and lonely leaves on naked branches trembling under the inclement skies, our spirits may become oppressed. Deliver us from this mood. Make us thankful for the maturing sun conspiring with the frosts to "fill all fruit with ripeness to the core," for the squirrel snug with his accomplished winter store and for the husbandman and housewife insured against hunger and cold through the coming months. Make us glad in the contemplation of Autumn's pageant of yellow and bronze, of crimson and gold. Who can paint like Nature, O Lord? And what canvasses she hangs in October's gallery! "Day unto day uttereth speech, And night unto night showeth knowledge," and all Thy works praise Thee in all seasons and all places of Thy dominion! Amen.

†

CHILDLIKENESS

I thank thee, O Father, Lord of heaven and earth, that thou didst hide these things from the wise and understanding, and didst reveal them unto babes –Matthew 11:25

We thank Thee, our Father, that there is a heaven of difference between being "childish" and "childlike." May we not miss the truth that Jesus was once a child and from that estate "grew in wisdom and stature and in favour with God and man." May we catch the lesson He would teach when "he set a young child in the midst of his disciples." We know that our lives are often sordid, because we are lacking in the pure affection of childhood; our eyes blind, because we have lost the fine sensitiveness of the young; and our minds hard and set instead of open and alert, because we are not full of their eager questionings. Give us today a new birth of the spirit of the little child. Help us to see that we are all but beginners in Eternity's great school, mere children, dependent upon a Parent who has never failed. Give us the child's trust, the child's wonder, the child's responsiveness and affection. In the Name of the Holy Child of Bethlehem. Amen.

CHILDREN'S DAY

And he took a little child, and set him in the midst of them —Mark 9:36

We know, heavenly Father, that Thy surprising and perfect fatherhood is the final explanation of why we have a day in each year devoted to thought of our children, and why all the days of the year are consecrated to our boys and girls as they are nowhere else outside of Christendom. Accept our thanks for our beloved children. How our thoughts center upon them as our lives are lived over again in them! God, keep them stainless and pure. May they grow strong and wise. May they help their fellows and walk with Thee, their God. Our hearts burn within us when we think of those who for gain would make spoil of these fair young lives. Oh, the monstrous daring of men's hearts that they should cause even one of these little ones to stumble. Arise, O Lord, and let the enemies of our children be scattered! May He who bade children come to Him rally to their cause and defend them against a thousand wiles of the devil. Give us more unselfish motherhood and fatherhood, that we may not enjoy our children as a luxury, but accept them as a holy trust from God. In Jesus' Name. Amen.

OUR CHILDREN

I was a son unto my father,
Tender and only beloved in the sight of my mother —Proverbs 4:3

Help us who are parents to realize how Godlike it is to be fathers and mothers. Thou art the perfect Parent. Thou dost neither slumber nor sleep; so watchful is Thy love. Thou dost attend to us in person and not relegate us to angels, however wise they might be. O God, we desire to be like Thy parental pattern. As these children are more to us than life itself, impress upon us that we must live true, kindly, and gracious lives for their sakes. In parental sacrifice may we bring them to honorable manhood and womanhood. May love be the crowning reality of our homes. We beseech Thee, Holy Spirit of God, so to guide and bless our youth that by and by they shall be marked by a mature integrity and humility, and a likeness to our Saviour. We ask in Jesus' Name. Amen.

THE CHRIST CHILD

Unto us a child is born, unto us a son is given
—Isaiah 9:6

Father in heaven, though in many places the earth is frost-bound, the trees are bare, and the landscape is desolate, yet in our hearts flowers are blossoming and birds are singing, because the beauty of Thy love has burst upon the world in the birth of the Infant Redeemer. Truly the light of heaven plays about the face of Mary's Child, reflecting the unclouded purity and the beauteous benignity of the Eternal. How strange and mysterious that in His gaze the innocence and helplessness of babyhood should somehow be blended with the emotions of infinite holiness and love. May Thy Infant Presence prove again to us the power of the weak things to overcome the things that are mighty. May the deep, abysmal better selves in us arise and rebuke the harsh, the sordid, the ignoble selves which rule us, and may we become again as little children, quick to forget injuries, eager to learn, and strong in faith. In Thy blessed Name. Amen.

CHRISTMAS

And she shall bring forth a son; and thou shalt call his name Jesus; for it is he that shall save his people from their sins – Matthew 1:21

Blessed Father of all men, may each son of Thine determine in this season of good-will to be a brother to someone in need. May many heartbreaks now be healed. May all who dwell in loneliness feel a human touch in their comfortless lives. Through brotherhood's beautiful ministry, may a glint of heaven's glory and God's steady love shine at least for an instant in the leaden skies of the forlorn. Make us human and tender. Melt our hardness. Show us that we are built for each other. May the "Merry Christmas" of our lips be touched with a tender cadence because it springs from a sincere heart, and may it be a benediction. Oh, may Christian fraternity, human sympathy, mutual helpfulness, and full forgiveness mark these coming days as never before. May it be the best Christmas of our lives. In the Name of the Holy Child. Amen.

CHRISTMAS

It came to pass, when the angels went away from them into heaven, the shepherds said one to another, let us now go even unto Bethlehem, and see this thing that is come to pass, which the Lord hath made known unto us – Luke 2:15

Hallow the thoughts of every heart, O Lord, as we consider the birth of our Infant Redeemer. May the social joys of this festive season not eclipse the brighter hopes of heavenly things which shine from the manger-cradle. Oh, wonderful meeting-place here of the Joy of God and the Joy of Man! Oh, wonderful summing-up in the tiny body of the Holy Child of the infinite love of the Everlasting Father! Such sanctifying of motherhood, such beautifying of childhood, such sure prophecy of purified manhood! Little child, Thou wast, and yet the master of the centuries! Thy tiny form lay warm upon Mary's heart, and at last we learned that the whole race of men lies near and dear on the Father's bosom. Good-will was the theme of the angels' music, for Thou wast the Prince of Peace. Let Thy glorious light shine from zone to zone. Break down prejudice. Fill the starved heart of the world with the peace and love and joy which it craves. Welcome, Christmas Day! Welcome, Babe Divine! We shall receive Thee joyfully in every home and heart! Amen.

CHRISTMAS LIVING

Love one another from the heart fervently – I Peter 1:22

With grateful and loving hearts we bless Thee, O Lord God, that Thou didst send a little Child to be cradled in Mary's arms, and His name was called Wonderful, Counselor, Mighty God, Everlasting Father, and Prince of Peace. Thou hast made us sure that eternal love is revealed in Jesus, Thy beloved Son. Make that love to shine anew at this Christmastime in many souls all around the world. Purge every heart from hard thoughts toward others or ungrateful thoughts toward Thee. Bless and hallow our Christmas mirth. May there be no pride in our giving and no envy in our receiving. May we send portions to them for whom nothing is prepared. May merry comradeship with those who are here be accompanied by good wishes and affectionate thought for those who are away; and may we remember again our oneness with all those who acknowledge Thee as Father and Jesus as Friend and Saviour. So may the Christmas bells chime in our hearts and the good-will music of the angels echo again upon our lips. In Jesus' Name. Amen.

THE SPIRIT OF CHRISTMAS

On earth peace, good will toward men

– Luke 2:14

We thank Thee, heavenly Father, for the beautifying and sweetening of life which Christmas brings. May we yield ourselves to the Presence that walks among us during this glad season. Spirit of the Holy Child, make every heart tender. Shed radiance in the darkest places, Stand beside sickbeds to comfort. Warm hearts that are forlorn. Minister through generous hands in every place of misery. May unmusical hearts break forth into song. May the spiritually color-blind have a sense of beauty. Quicken to a new and surprising humanity even the hearts of those who are naturally selfish. So may Christmas be more than a feast or a story or a holiday. May it bring a thrill of love for God and for our neighbor, yea, for our enemy and the race. In the Name of Him who was born in Bethlehem of Judea, who went about doing good and who died and rose again for our salvation. Amen.

COMFORT

For as the sufferings of Christ abound unto us, even so our comfort also aboundeth through Christ —II Corinthians 1:5

O God and Father of us all, soothe the anxieties of Thy children. Wherever there is disorder instead of calm, wherever there is burden instead of buoyancy, wherever there is fever instead of peace, there be Thou to touch, to guide, to encourage, to empower. O Lord, save Thy people. Enable us to take up again the weary task. Help us to bear the pettiness of people, the misunderstandings, and the incompatible natures. Perhaps the fault is in ourselves. Possibly we have wrestled with conscience till we have grieved and nearly quenched the Holy Spirit. We call unto Thee, O God, because "the spirit is willing, but the flesh is weak." Rescue us, through Him, whom in our inmost souls, we know to be the only Saviour of the world. Amen.

COMFORT

Their soul melteth away because of trouble. . . .
And are at their wits' end.
Then they cry unto Jehovah in their trouble,
And He bringeth them out of their distresses
—Psalm 107:26, 27, 28

O Lord, our Lord, how excellent is Thy name in all the earth!" We thank Thee for the morning light, daily reminder of the Sun of Righteousness, risen "with healing in his wings." We thank Thee for the revelation of Thyself in the works of Nature: for the rapture of singing birds that challenges our praise and puts a new song in our mouths, for blooming flowers that arouse within us pure desires to be clad in the beauty of holiness. If we are dwelling in gloom because of real or fancied evil, if we are morbid and self-condemning because of our spiritual defeats, if we are oppressed by the cares of business, home or official responsibility, if we are sorrowing for a dear one – minister to us comfort and peace in such abundant measure as to surprise us with Thy love and to enable us to rise and stand upon our feet to face the world and our duties again through Jesus Christ who strengtheneth us. Amen.

EASTER

Lo, I am with you always, even unto the end of the world –Matthew 28:20.

O living Lord, not only do our thoughts at Eastertide turn to our hope of immortality which was confirmed when Thou didst walk forth from the grave, but they turn to Thee as walking evermore with Thy people on earth just as Thou didst with Mary in the garden and with the two on the way to Emmaus. What a wondrous form we should behold if we were in utter spiritual harmony with Thee! As the radio catches melody, present in the air but without its aid unheard, so, if our faculties were enhanced enough by Thy Holy Spirit, we should actually behold the King in His beauty and hear His voice. Although we cannot as yet see the glorified body of our Saviour, may we believe in His unfailing presence, for He said, "Lo! I am with you always, even unto the end of the world." May we walk and talk with Him; may we rely upon Him. So may Easter Day not pass without leaving to many, as a perpetual blessing, the constant companionship of Him "whom having not seen we love." Amen.

EASTER

"But the truth is, Christ was raised to life – the first-fruits of the harvest of the dead.

I Corinthians 15:20.

O Thou, who art the ever-living Lord, we acknowledge how weak and finite we are, for we know that we are all tending toward inevitable decay and the final moment of our lives, and we sometimes tremble at the unknown Beyond. But today our fears are hushed and our hopes triumph as we join the Apostles and the saintly women in the glad wonder of Easter. We bless Thee for the disk of rock revolving in its groove, the opened tomb, the King in His beauty walking among the lilies of the garden, the women in an ecstasy of surprise and joy, the disciples racing to the tomb and finding it untenanted by the shrouded form that lay upon its rocky shelf, the Resurrection of the Redeemer! "Christ the first fruits, afterward they that are Christ's at his coming" – the waving of the single sheaf before the Lord, pattern and pledge of the glorious human harvest which shall one day wave over all the fields of God. May all the bewildered, sorrowing and desolate wrap the Easter thought around their sore and weary hearts so that cold and cheerless habitations may glow with warmth; that the "empty chair" may somehow lose its power to depress; that no one may have any dread of taking the returnless path himself, but comfort and calm may displace sorrow, and courage and peace may expel fear. "Therefore let us be stedfast, unmovable, always abounding in the work of the Lord, forasmuch as we know that our labour is not in vain in the Lord." Amen.

THE EASTER VICTORY

Jesus said, . . . I am the resurrection, and the life
—John 11:25.

Strong Son of God, immortal Love, Victor over death and the grave, we rejoice that the satanic malignity of proud Pharisees and ruthless Romans was utterly futile. No tomb could hold Thee, though Thou wast weakened on a cruel cross, stabbed with a Roman spear and sealed unto darkness by a ponderous disk of stone. Thy persecutors were not fighting against mere flesh and blood, for "in him dwelleth all the fulness of the Godhead bodily, who is the head of all principality and power." At the cemetery we repeat the words, "O death, where is thy sting? O grave, where is thy victory?" And, as we follow our Lord Jesus to the glory of Easter morning, we recall His majestic words, "I was dead, and behold, I am alive for evermore." May the Holy Spirit move more present-day followers of Christ to dedicate themselves to Jesus Christ in the wholehearted devotion of the sainted Eleven, who gave up their very lives for His sake. Amen.

EASTER EVENING

Why art thou cast down, O my soul?
And why art thou disquieted within me?
Hope thou in God; for I shall yet praise him,
Who is the help of my countenance, and my God.
—Psalm 42:11

O Spirit of the living God, breathe upon us as Jesus breathed upon His friends in the upper room on Easter night, saying, "Receive ye the Holy Ghost." Without Thee we can do nothing. Our lives are too often marked by sloth, by pride, by self-satisfaction, by apathy. We are sluggards in the spiritual realm. But Thine ear is not heavy that it cannot hear nor Thine arm shortened that it cannot save. "All things are possible with God." Speak to us through the Holy Spirit, the conscience, the Scriptures, or a human messenger, and let the valley of dry bones be transformed. May hidden powers of initiative, conquest, fruitfulness, dedication, and assurance of religious faith be made known to us till we rise from the dead and walk hand in hand with the Master. In Jesus' Name. Amen.

X EASTER'S AFTERGLOW

Fear not; I am the first and the last, and the Living one; and I was dead, and behold, I am alive for evermore. —Revelation 1:17, 18

Lord of our life and God of our salvation, Thou hast once more "brought life and immortality to light" out of the garden tomb. We have followed the Master to His cross. We have seen the cross become His throne, even as He said, "I, if I be lifted up, will draw all men unto me." We bless Thee for that mastery of men which began with the adoring exclamation of the centurion and which has widened with the process of the suns until it has reached our own shores. We bless Thee for the sway over all humanity and the rule of our own lives which Jesus exercises "more and more unto the perfect day." His victory over death and His promise to make us "more than conquerors" gives us a great hope that virtue will finally conquer vice, that the sweet will ultimately replace the bitter, that light will eventually flood all darkness, and that God's ways which are "higher than our ways" will at last be accepted on earth as they are in heaven. Now give us, O Lord, patience, courage, goodwill and charity to labor on, each in his own place, "always abounding in the work of the Lord, forasmuch as we know that [our] labor is not in vain in the Lord." In His Name. Amen.

POST-EASTER

I know him whom I have believed, and I am persuaded that he is able to guard that which I have committed unto him against that day
—II Timothy 1:12.

Now that Easter is past and gone, O Father, let not the quickened hope which it brought leave us as we take up the everyday cares of life again. How many of us, Thou knowest, seem to have most of our treasures in heaven: those whom we have "loved and lost long since awhile." And yet have we not learned that love is loveliest when spoken in tears? Help us, while Easter's assurance is still with us, to assert our faith. "What can shake our sure repose?" We rely utterly on Him who said, "If it were not so I would have told you." We know He will never disappoint us. Our loved ones are not shades, apparitions, unreal. *Ours* is the dream-life, theirs the *reality.* And so, O God, we believe and are sure that some day we shall again be "imparadised in one another's arms." Lord, increase our faith. Amen.

†

POST-EASTER

Jesus Christ . . . gave himself for our sins, that he might deliver us out of this present evil world, according to the will of our God and Father . . . who raised him from the dead
—Galatians 1:1, 4, 1.

Our heavenly Father, our hearts are stirred with a new devotion to Jesus as we come to think of His last week on earth. We marvel at the way in which He foiled those who disputed with Him but bowed to those who crucified Him. We wonder at His virile resistance of hypocrisy combined with His meek forgiveness of enemies. We are amazed, O Lord, at the agony in the Garden and yet more amazed as He overcame His human weakness and moved forward to the cross. We bless Thee for Easter's pledge of everlasting life with ever new intimacies of friendship with Thee and all our brother men, with new ascents of knowledge to climb, with ever new worlds of thought and experience and achievement to conquer, with all separation and death behind us, with pain gone, with tears dried, with failures impossible, with sin unknown, and all men gathered about Thee, bound with golden chains of love. Bring us, O Lord, to that fair country. Amen.

COMMENCEMENT

He maketh me to lie down in green pastures;
He leadeth me beside still waters.
He restoreth my soul:
He guideth me in the paths of righteousness for his name's sake

—Psalm 23:2, 3.

O God, as Thou art our Father, thou knowest how parents' love is fashioned after Thine. We cannot always utter in words the way we feel about our children, but we thank Thee for the opportunities we have had to express our affection for them in deeds, and to bring them to their graduation day. Our hearts sing with them in the joy of Commencement season. And we would pray for them too. Although they are our boys and girls, yet each is also Thy child. Our heavenly Father, Thou hast a high and holy plan for each. Help these, our beloved, to find and keep Thy way. May they never miss their high destiny. They are necessary to Thee, though Thou art Almighty. In all their ways may they acknowledge Thee, that Thou mayest direct them in their paths. Amen.

COMMENCEMENT

Only be strong and very courageous, to observe to do according to all the law, which Moses my servant commanded thee: turn not from it to the right hand or to the left —Joshua 1:7.

O God, who dost give strength to the weak and courage to those who face new ways, grant them that they may both know and do according to Thy commandment. Give them, O Lord, courage to choose the High Way with Thee. Give to these Thy children that they may walk in newness of life in Christ Jesus. Grant them that wisdom which comes down from on high, splendid courage for hard tasks, and endurance for the more humble position. May each know that the worker glorifies his work. O, loving heavenly Father, inspire them to start each day with Thee, rest them in their toil, and when night comes, may they give back to Thee a well-spent day. O Thou who hast promised to be the Companion of all their days and all their ways, wherever their feet may be found, may they know the conscious fellowship of the Christ of God who said: "Lo, I am with you always, even unto the end of the world." In Christ's Name. Amen.

COMMENCEMENT

I [Wisdom] love them that love me;
And those that seek me diligently shall find me
—Proverbs 8:17.

We offer Thee, O Lord, our song of thanksgiving for the schools of the nation. Thou hast made tax-payers generous, parents self-sacrificing, governing educational bodies far-seeing and devoted; teachers wise, and students earnest. The eye and cheek of youth are beautiful to us today. We bless Thee for all that improvement which the years in our schools and colleges have made. Show us how to enrich our teaching program that we may teach our students how to educate themselves, how to attain broader mental outlooks, and how to realize spiritual objectives. Give us teachers who dominate by personality rather than by force. Keep all guides of youth from being mere framers of definitions and inventors of techniques, and show them how to add to knowledge, inspiration, and to inspiration, outlook, and to outlook, uplook, until our students shall possess the invaluable endowment of faith in God. In Jesus' Name. Amen.

†

COMMENCEMENT

He took upon Him the form of a servant . . . [and] went about doing good

Philippians 2:7 and Acts 10:38

O Father of lights and Fountain of all knowledge, we bring to Thee our work as the end of the school year approaches: tax-payers and donors have done their part; parents have sacrificed; teachers have shown a sense of their high stewardship, and many students have been industrious. We pray that Thou wilt crown the year's task with Thy favor. As teachers have tried not so much to cram the head with knowledge as to unfetter the spirit of young manhood and young womanhood so that it should face the world undaunted, to produce self-respect and courage in the presence of temptation and difficulties, and to endow with insight and judgment, may our graduates perceive the true objective of life. May they understand that Thy measurements are in terms of usefulness to society. May they never take their eyes off Him, "who took upon him the form of a servant, and went about doing good." Amen

FOR STUDENTS

Wisdom shall enter into thy heart,
And knowledge shall be pleasant unto thy soul
—Proverbs 2:10

We are grateful, O Lord our King, that America with all its "getting" is endeavoring so mightily to "get understanding." Our hearts are thrilled once more at the sight of the opening schools, colleges and universities. We bless Thee for the sacrifices of loving parents, and of childless citizens, too, in providing facilities for education unmatched in all the history of the world. And now we would dedicate our youth to Thee. Their strength and their achievement are in Thy keeping. Show them where wisdom hides her perennial springs of freshness and sweetness. Make of them gentle, patient scholars, useful, honorable citizens, and followers of God. May their lives be kept unblemished by any evil thing. Touch their eyes with vision to perceive their priceless opportunity in the year that is just ahead. In Jesus' Name. Amen.

THE SCHOOLS

He . . . appointed a law . . .,
Which he commanded our fathers,
That they should make them known to their children . . .;
That they might set their hope in God . . .
And . . . keep his commandments.
—Psalm 78:5, 7

Heavenly Father, America's voice rises in prayer to Thee to bless its great establishment of education. As our schools are opening once more, we commend them to Thy gracious care and guidance. Our youth seek a larger life, new knowledge that will lead to better development of the human spirit, better social adjustment, and understanding of Thee. Bless the great host of men and women consecrated to the task of instruction. Through them as through fair windows, let the light, broad as truth itself, pour into their students. May all the "forces of the firmament fortify the strength" of the teachers and the taught. Show them which are the half truths and which are the whole. May inexperience be guided in the paths of wisdom by a wisdom ever seeking new heights itself. May our youth covet earnestly the best gifts and be eager and industrious in the presence of their great opportunity, and may multitudes of them, like Mary, be found "sitting at the feet of Jesus," the greatest Teacher of all. In His Name. Amen.

THE SCHOOLS OPEN AGAIN

Say not, I am a child; for to whomsoever I shall send thee thou shalt go, and whatsoever I shall command thee thou shalt speak —Jeremiah 1:7

Heavenly Father, we pray for Thy blessing upon America's whole establishment of learning from the kindergarten to the university. We acknowledge with humble thanks that in Thy good providence, our youth have advantages of education never known before. May the younger generation use the new instrument of science guided by the old impulses of faith in such a way as to correct many of the age-old errors of the past. With independence and courage may they assess at its true value their inheritance. Standing upon the firm ground of reality and truth, may they challenge the pessimism of those who say the world never changes, and may they fare forth upon their generation's task. Keep them from undesirable tangents, but keep them also from the old well-trodden and unproductive circle. Show them how to keep their feet upon the Rock and to establish their goings in the direction of real progress. In the Name of the Young Man of Galilee. Amen.

WHEN SCHOOLS OPEN

Let us give ourselves to our ministry; or he that teacheth, to his teaching" —Romans 12:7.

Great Teacher of Mankind, we turn to Thee with gratitude as we think of the troops of young people who are now storming again the gates of our schoolhouses, and as we remember the great host of men and women who are giving their lives to the instruction of these boys and girls. Bless our teachers in their labor of love. When we think of the responsibility of their task we are moved to pray that they may have a special measure of Divine aid. Enable them to give the knowledge upon which sound citizenship is based and to build the moral fiber which such citizenship demands. May they make the school an effective organ for the cultivation of community spirit and national consciousness. May they be able to arouse multitudes of youth from mental stupor and moral inertness and give them an impulse to understand the frame of life and fit themselves helpfully into it. So through our schools, Almighty Regent, be pleased to bring about the triumph of reason and the kingdom of love. In the Name of the Teacher of Galilee. Amen.

AWARENESS OF GOD

Awake, thou that sleepest, and arise from the dead, and Christ shall shine upon thee
—Ephesians 5:14

O Thou blessed Father of our spirits, help us to be still and know that Thou art God. May Thy Spirit arouse us from our dullness and coldness, and put into our minds the thrilling thought of the unspeakable love Thou hast for us. O Holy Father, if we knew how near Thou art, we would remove the shoes from our feet, knowing that the place whereon we stand is holy ground. Give us that hush that befits those so wondrously fashioned, so divinely accompanied and so mysteriously destined. Give us that divine nature which shall triumph over time and sense and matter; which shall deliver us from things coarse and vain and unspiritual; which shall promote within us every pure sentiment, all urgency and sweetness of true affection, and all diligence in the King's business; and send us out in the paths of Him who went about doing good. In Jesus' Name. Amen.

THE FAMILY OF GOD

Holy Father, keep them in thy name which thou hast given me, that they may be one, even as we are —John 17:11

O Lord, how vast is Thy creation! As we think of the birds of the air, the fish of the sea, of every creeping thing on the earth, and of man whom Thou hast made in Thy image, we adore Thee anew and exclaim, "How great Thou art!" As Thou dost regard so tenderly Thine infinite brood, grant to us, we pray Thee, consideration, restraint, and charity, that we may regard all men, even our bitter enemies and the faraway multitudes as well as our friends and neighbors, as those who are dear to Thee. Thou art the God of the erring as well as the true, of the invalid as well as the vigorous, of the prisoner as well as the free. O bless all mankind with a greater sense of its unity. May we be loyal to each other in all the relationships of life in spite of occasions of discord. May we be so bound to Thee that division shall seem to us a disease. Help us to abhor all taint and selfishness and corruption which breed ill will and strife. Help us to be one and to fulfill Jesus' prayer in the Garden. In His Name. Amen.

GOD CARES

I have loved thee with an everlasting love
—Jeremiah 31:3

No matter what happens, O Lord, help us not to lose our faith in Thee. May we never give way to the belief that Thou art hard and unfeeling or helpless in the bondage of iron laws Thou hast made. Though we have failed in our undertakings and are mocked by our fellows, though health has broken and years of pain are ahead, though the light has gone out of our homes, though "the arrows of outrageous fortune" have pierced us through and through, yet may we trustfully "endure as seeing him who is invisible." We thank Thee that the great Sufferer offers us His company, and that the consolations of David and Job and Isaiah and John and Paul are ours. Help us to discover hidden meanings in misfortune, sorrow, and loss. And when we cannot explain, help us still to trust. Thou, O God, hast proved Thyself through the ages. We believe that Thou art love, and we will trust Thee forever and ever. All praise to Thee, the Triune God. Amen.

GOD HELPS US

Out of weakness were made strong, waxed valiant in fight —Hebrews 11:34.

O Lord, we are thankful for the teaching of Thy Word that out of weakness we may be made strong; and we are grateful that our experience has shown the truth of the promise. Thou givest aim and direction to lives that have been feeble and uncertain. Thou dost bring up from the depths of being powerful emotions to take the place of shallow, commonplace thinking. Thou dost reconcile flesh and spirit and other warring powers of our natures and through Thy Holy Spirit dost unite our hearts in Thy love and in human service. Impart, we pray Thee, the gallantry and courage of a knight. May we be enabled to say with David, "By thee I run upon a troop. And by my God do I leap over a wall." In the Name of the Lion of the Tribe of Judah. Amen.

GOD IN MAN

In him we live, and move, and have our being
—Acts 17:28

O righteous Father, the world knew thee not." Thou art all about us, and within us, yet we do not recognize Thee. "The ox knoweth its owner and the ass its master's crib" – but Thine own sons and daughters are not always aware of Thee. How tragic that some of us live whole stretches of years before we learn that Thou art pursuing us in loving desire, and hast been near us all along! Open our eyes that we may see Thee everywhere in the human life about us. May we find Thee in all the noble activities of men: may we see the outreach of Thine arm when the needy are supplied, the passion of Thy soul when men strive to relieve their fellows from oppression, the eternal faithfulness of the Divine in every human deed of self-sacrifice. Thou dost live and move and have Thy being in men. May we see Thee present and active in our midst as well as in the ages past or in the hidden heavens today. Thou art right at hand. Give us faith to reach out and touch Thee. For Jesus' sake. Amen.

GOD IS LOVE

Oh send out thy light and thy truth; let them lead me;
Let them bring me unto thy holy hill,
And to thy tabernacles.
Then will I go unto the altar of God

—Psalm 43:3

Our Father, Thou knowest how often we turn from faith to doubt and again from despair to hope. We thank Thee for our vision-moments when "God's in His heaven and all's well with the world" and we pray that our lives may be made pure that we may have this vision of Thee, not as a fleeting glimpse of the Divine but as a daily and hourly peace that passes all understanding. We thank Thee for Jesus, the gracious and tender-hearted, the One who was in Himself the express image of Thee, the outshining of Thy glory. Give us the spirit of little children who repent quickly, are forgiven often, and received always because of their simple trust. If we have been prodigals far from home, help some of us today to say, "I will arise and go unto my Father." In the Name of His blessed Son. Amen.

THE GOD OF HOPE

Now the God of hope fill you with all joy and peace in believing —Romans 15:13

O Thou, the Keeper of Israel, a very present help in trouble, Thou makest hope to spring eternal in the human breast. If any of us are laboring under a sense of failure, if duties have been left undone, if we have yielded to temptation, may we remember the returning prodigal and how when he was yet a great way off his father saw him and had compassion and ran and fell on his neck and kissed him. Give us such faith that we shall march straight home to Thee. If hardship has crushed nature's loveliness out of us, if hopeless debt has robbed our peace, if all our brave songs of yesterday have turned into cries of pain and need, may we have the assurance that Thy heart is broken for the hopeless sorrows and burdens of Thy people and may we answer the call of Him who said, "Come unto me, all ye that labor and are heavy laden." Though He then bids us take His "yoke" upon us, may we learn that only by helping others shall we find help and by cheering others shall we find cheer. In Jesus' Name. Amen.

GOD'S GOOD NEWS

The opening of thy words giveth light
—Psalm 119:130

We thank Thee that in this world of sorrow and sin, of misfortune and heartache, of pain and disease, there is a Book whose constant message is a word of hope. We bless Thee that when sorrow calls for consolation it never disappoints and that when earth's wearied travelers thirst for eternal waters it is a fountain of perennial sweetness and satisfaction. We thank Thee that it breaks prisoners' chains, exposes hypocrisy, dries tears, points heavenward, elevates civilization, exalts love, and regenerates human hearts. "The opening of thy words giveth light." "Open our eyes to behold wondrous things out of thy law." May those who understand the unutterable values of this Book help to make its influence increase not so much by answering with elaborate briefs the ranting of destructive critics and cynics as by demonstrating in their lives the truths which the Bible proclaims. In the Name of Him who said, "Search the scriptures." Amen.

†

GOD'S PURSUING LOVE

Surely the darkness shall cover me; even the night shall be light about me. Yea, the darkness hideth not from thee; but the night shineth as the day: the darkness and the light are both alike to thee —Psalm 139:11, 12.

Our heavenly Father, we marvel at the great love wherewith Thou hast loved us. We are foolish and try at times to break away from Thy hand and run into danger, but Thou dost hold us fast. We say we will have nothing to do with Thee, but Thou dost continue to make Thy sun to shine on the evil as well as the good. "Thou dost send thy rain on the just and the unjust also." Thou art not working merely in or through the Church, but Thou goest everywhere; among publicans and sinners, wrestling with the wayward, and among haters of men, "making the wrath of men to praise thee." Whoever we are and wherever we are, if our senses were keener, O Lord, we should feel Thee "like the wind upon our cheeks, like the tide about the shore, like a hand within our own." O Love unchanging, help us now to yield to Thee. Amen.

GOD'S WILLINGNESS

If ye then, being evil, know how to give good gifts unto your children, how much more shall your father who is in heaven give good things to them that ask him?" –Matthew 7:11

Truly, O God, "Thou openest thy hand and satisfiest the desire of every living thing." Thou art ever waiting to be gracious. The fault is with us. We neglect Thy love. We turn away from the Strength that would steady and from the Hand that would save. We shut ourselves out from the radiance, the life, and the songs of the redeemed. Help us to look back and recall what God did with Moses when he overcame his hesitation and put himself under Divine direction, and what He did with Paul when he stopped resisting the conscience within him and surrendered to Jesus Christ. And may we also look forward to the end when the things of time and sense will seem small as we stand on the circle of the spheres before the Almighty. In view of that solemn reality may we heed Thy call, "Today, if any man will hear my voice, harden not your hearts" and may we begin to live lives that are honest, helpful and pure. In Jesus' Name. Amen.

THE REVEALER OF GOD

No man hath seen God at any time; the only begotten Son, who is in the bosom of the Father, he hath declared him. –John 1:18

O God, infinite, eternal and unchangeable, we know full well that we do not view Thee from the eternal arches of infinity but from the lowly angles of earth. We know that Thou art a Spirit and that Thou art timeless and spaceless. We know that the order of Thy being, the beauty, love and perfection of Thy nature must be beyond the mind of man to conceive. And yet, though we cannot pierce the veil where Thy unimagined glory dwelleth, we thank Thee that we have caught Thy reflected image in Jesus Christ. We thank Thee for His unspeakably illuminating and comforting saying, "He that hath seen me hath seen the Father." We thank Thee that, in Jesus, God stated Himself so plainly that a child may know Him. Give us the childlike heart. Give us faith. Give us trust. Give us filial love. Make us happy and hopeful, free and strong, as we rejoice in Him who has loved us with an everlasting love. Through Him who is "Jesus, Lover of our souls." Amen.

ANTI-SPIRIT ATTITUDES

Grieve not the Holy Spirit – Ephesians 4:30
Quench not the Spirit – I Thessalonians 5:19
Ye do always resist the Holy Spirit – Acts 7:51

We are grateful, O Lord, that the Holy Spirit is not like a traffic officer or a drill sergeant who asserts his superiority and issues sharp orders, but that He is rather "the still small voice" that spoke to Elijah and the noiseless dovelike One who descended upon Jesus at His baptism. We thank Thee that He displays celestial meekness, and appeals to us by encouraging suggestions instead of by a hard series of solemn injunctions. But may we realize that it is within our power to repulse the Spirit and thus lose all His benefits. Rather, may we make the Holy Spirit feel at home in our hearts. May we ever regard Him as a Being of heavenly tenderness and of infinite energy whose steps within us are as noiseless as a snowflake reaching the earth. May we never grieve, quench or resist this Holy One. Thus may He be free to encourage and fortify us in every good word and deed. Through Jesus Christ, our Lord. Amen.

FILLED WITH THE SPIRIT

I bow my knees unto the Father . . . that he would grant you . . . that ye may be strengthened with power through his Spirit in the inward man
—Ephesians 3:14

O Lord, may we not be half-in-half Christians, but may we accept the challenge, "Be ye filled with the Spirit." May we not resemble a hotel with many empty rooms, but one with every room occupied, and all taken by the One blessed Guest, the Holy Spirit. May there be no preferred occupants known as Pleasure, Business, or Ambition. May we recall the bitter regret of Joseph and Mary when "there was no room for them in the inn," and realize the similar sorrow of the Spirit when the most private and precious precincts of our hearts are denied to Him. Help us, O God, to be filled with the Spirit and thus to face danger like Peter and Paul, to overcome hatred like Stephen, and to smother ingrained prejudice like Barnabas. May we join the company of Elisabeth, Zacharias, Simeon and John the Baptist who were said to be "filled with the Spirit." We pray in the Name of Him who bequeathed the Comforter. Amen.

THE SOURCE OF POWER

Ye shall receive power, when the Holy Spirit is come upon you —Acts 1:8

We bless Thy Name, our Father, that Jesus, before concluding His visible ministry in our world, promised His disciples "I will pray the Father and he shall give you another Comforter." And how richly did the Holy Spirit fulfill this promise! We have Him to thank that in the ancient world of godless myths and philosophies which were but speculation only, the belief in our Divine Lord took root, blossomed, and the glorious fruit of the Spirit began to appear in the earth. Men gradually turned from unparalled pride, cruelty, self-indulgence in lust, drink, and gluttony, to form a fellowship of the Christ. We thank Thee that down to these latter days the indwelling Spirit has shown us also how to avoid the bad of every kind, how to follow Christ, and how to put God first in every thought, word, and deed. May the fruit of the Spirit which issues in love, joy, and peace be unmistakably found in our lives. In the Name of our Lord Jesus. Amen.

THE SPIRIT'S OFFICES

The harvest of the Spirit is love, joy, peace, patience, kindness, goodness, fidelity, gentleness and self-control —Galatians 5:22, 23.

Thou hast proven Thyself, O Lord, "the Giver of every good and perfect gift," inasmuch as Thou hast bestowed the Holy Spirit to help poor erring mortals to aspire to the upper realm. We thank Thee for His many invaluable offices as Thy Premier of Paradise, to inspire men like Moses and David and Paul with messages direct from the eternal mind as contained in the Bible, to keep in perpetual circulation the life-giving words of our Lord, and to transmit spiritual power from the skies enabling men to overcome the wiles of Satan. Truly "to them who have no might he increaseth strength." We even do not know what we should pray for as we ought, but, through our inarticulate groans, the Spirit Himself is pleading for us and God knows what the Spirit means. So we bless and magnify Thy Holy Name, the blessed Three in One, "the same in substance, equal in power and glory." Amen.

BETHANY

And he left them, and went forth out of the city to Bethany, and lodged there – Matthew 21:17

Our Heavenly Father, as the days draw near when we meditate upon the controversies and the sufferings of the last terrible week of Jesus' life, we thank Thee for Bethany where He, the Master, found evening by evening the friendship that enabled Him day by day to meet the envy and spleen of those whose hypocrisy He exposed. We thank Thee for His good friends Mary and Martha and Lazarus. Remind us of Mary's memorial in His honor. It is a comfort to us, O Lord, to recall that whereas "there was no room for him in the inn" where he was born, there was a beautiful home to which He could go every night in the final week of His life, and there was a tomb bravely proffered wherein His suffering body, white and spent, might be received. Oh, for the coming of a day when it shall not be a vain summons to sing, "Let every heart prepare Him room"! Amen.

MARY OF BETHANY

Mary therefore took a pound of ointment of pure spikenard, very precious, and anointed the feet of Jesus, and wiped his feet with her hair
—John 12:3

As the Lenten meditations of Thy people approach the final Passion of our Lord, we pause to wonder and to bless Thee for the swift, spontaneous act of a woman who loved Jesus in the strength of a pure and exalted passion. We thank Thee for the gift of the alabaster box of ointment poured upon His head — true symbol of a heart pouring out its love. We bless Thee for the poise of Jesus as He received the tribute. Oh, the simplicity, grace, and courtesy of His nature! Oh, the wisdom of His teaching, that it is not waste to love and to dedicate to God, but that he who gives most to God will give most to men. We marvel at the unspeakable glory of Mary's deed, that when the hour for all earthly kindness to Jesus was passing fast away, it was given to a woman's sure intuition to know that flowers and praises for our dead are often fearful anomaly. While Jesus was alive Mary would show her love. O Lord, who knows how the piercing pain of the final agony was softened by her precious and gracious act? Give us devotion such as hers. In Thy Name. Amen.

†

PALM SUNDAY

And Jesus came to them and spake unto them saying, all authority hath been given unto me in heaven and in earth —Matthew 28:18

O Holy Sovereign of the world, we would join the ancient marchers who acclaimed Thy Triumphal Entry and could contain themselves in their joy no longer, but threw love-gifts of apparel and greenery in Thy way as Thou didst enter Jerusalem. Thou art forever, before all time and on earth and in eternity to come, King of kings and Lord of lords. Didst Thou not declare, "I, if I lifted up, will draw all men unto me"? We bless Thee for the prophecy of Paul that the day is sure to come when "every tongue [shall] confess that Jesus Christ is Lord to the glory of God the Father." We would consecrate our means, our talents, our knowledge, our influence, our very reason for existence to the one great purpose that all Thy children of every race and clime and condition might come to know Thee and Jesus Christ, whom Thou, O God, didst send to be the world's Redeemer. Amen.

GETHSEMANE

And he said, Abba, Father, all things are possible unto thee; remove this cup from me: howbeit not what I will, but what thou wilt

— Mark 14:36

O Lord, it is easy for us to believe in life when all things go well with us — when youth and strength are ours, when we have happy friendships, and when we are making a success. But when hopes are disappointed, health breaks, dear ones are taken, and misfortune comes, then how many are ready to repudiate life rather than endure it. In the forlorn and unfriended hour may we remember Gethsemane. Although Jesus displayed no morbid desire for pain like some ascetics, yet we bless Thee, O God, for His solemn determination to see life through to its end and to endure to the uttermost. He shrank from the cup but drained it to the dregs. We praise Thee for the unseen helpers who supplemented His own human maximum of endurance. If in an intolerable hour any of us are asking the question, "Is life worth living?" may His endurance be a fortifying example, and may the strengthening angels who ministered to Him remind us that Heaven's help is always near, and we shall never be tried beyond our limit without higher powers being sent, in answer to our cry for help. In Jesus' Name. Amen.

CALVARY

In his own person he carried our sins to the gallows, so that we might cease to live for sin and begin to live for righteousness —I Peter 2:24.

Father of all grace and love, we have followed Thy Son our Saviour through the closing weeks of His life and are now come to the foot of His cross. Oh, the immortal bondage of humanity which was ended on Calvary – the lust of evil, the dread of judgment, the power of the devil, the clutch of superstition, the fear of death! Thou, our Saviour, didst "bring deliverance to the captive." Thou didst satisfy the violated law of holiness. We do not understand all the meanings of Thy sacrifice. We only know Thou didst die for us and that "the peace of God which passeth all understanding" has filled our hearts. Forbid, O Lord, that our experience should end in a sentiment however holy. Give us new perception and desire. Give us a new sympathy for our fellow men and a new faculty for service. May love and will and conscience be rooted in the life and love of our eternal Lord and blossom both on this side of the River and on that. In His Name. Amen.

THE MAN ON THE CROSS

Forasmuch then as Christ suffered in the flesh, arm ye yourselves also with the same mind
— I Peter 4:1

O God, our heavenly Father, shed light, we beseech Thee, during this Holy Week upon all those who suffer so keenly that they are tempted to doubt the existence of a God of love. Out of the depths they cry, "Is there a God in Israel?" When these dark thoughts assail Thy children's faith, oh, may they lift their eyes to the Man on the Cross. Thou hast suffered, too. We bless Thee for that picture which meets the inmost craving of our hearts. We shall never solve the problem of evil, but when we see Thy well-beloved Son nailed to the cruel cross, we understand that we are led through no darker rooms than Jesus, and that God knows the reason for pain and heartache and loss, even though we do not. In that faith may we stand beside Job and say, "Though he slay me, yet will I trust him," and echo the word of the Psalmist, "God is the strength of my heart, and my portion forever." In Jesus' Name. Amen.

THE CHRISTIAN HOME

The lines are fallen unto me in pleasant places
— Psalms 16:6

O God, we thank Thee for these little kingdoms that we call Home. Although full of problems and responsibilities, of drudgery and routine, yet they are our prime sources of happiness. Teach us to respect our homes, not as mere stopping-places, but as sacred institutions. May tired men find their homes a place of rest. By the very pathos of the Master's cry, "The Son of man hath not where to lay his head," may we gather new courage to assure our loved ones a haven of quiet waters, an asylum of safety and peace, a retreat of blessed relief from the Babel voices of the world. May these homes of ours quicken ambition, too. May they invigorate every member's desire to go out into the world and play a useful part. Wherever there is a father or a mother, a son or a daughter consciously making a brave, though unrecognized, effort to smooth, to sweeten, or to greaten the life of some home, let Thy hand of blessing rest there. In the Name of the Son of Mary. Amen.

THE CHRISTIAN HOME

My people shall abide in a peaceable habitation, and in safe dwellings, and in quiet resting-places
— Isaiah 32:18

Heavenly Father, Thou hast "set the solitary in families," and we bless Thee for the confidence that however many influences may conspire against the home, it can never be entirely supplanted by any device of man. We bless Thee that there is a place "where a world of strife can be shut out and a world of love shut in," where "the small are great and the great are small." We thank Thee for the background of quiet peace, or honor, affection, and personal tenderness which enables men to go out into a world that is often unreasonable, unfeeling, and rough. We bless Thee for the homes where, subtle and pervasive as the scent of lavender, is the sense of God's loving presence, and where there is retreat from struggles with the hard, uncaring world into the sweet security of eventide. May we never forget that Jesus spent thirty years at home and only three away. Amen.

THE CHRISTIAN HOME

As for me and my house, we will serve Jehovah
—Joshua 24:15

Help us to live, we beseech Thee, O Lord, so that if our houses were of glass and our words were broadcasted for the world to hear, we should be unashamed. May all parents recognize the high calling of parenthood and create a wholesome atmosphere for their children. As they see seductions surrounding youth on all sides, give them the grace and wisdom to prepare their young for clean and useful lives. Lord Jesus, remind mothers of the purity and beauty of Thy mother so that they may be stirred to seek a nobler type of womanhood, unsophisticated perhaps in the world's latest books, fashions, or amusements, but wise in the ways of love. Give us more fathers who are made of moral oak, who are centers of order in the home, who challenge the best aspirations of their sons when they ascend toward manhood. Guide our growing boys and girls in this day of their greater liberty. May they recognize the values of the sainted past as they try to bring in a better future. Deliver them from the snare of a new-found freedom by enabling them to fare forth only in that "liberty wherewith Christ hath made us free." In His Name. Amen.

THE CHRISTIAN HOME

And the ark of God remained . . . in his house . . .: and Jehovah blessed the house of Obed-edom, and all that he had
– I Chronicles 13:14

Lord Jesus, as we recall how Thou didst honor the godly home at Bethany and didst both give and receive spiritual refreshment there, we are sadly reminded of the difference between that happy and holy atmosphere and many of our own home circles. We are forced to admit that the Ark of the Covenant must compete with radios, air conditioners, appliances, and telephones. Thy ancient summons, "Learn of me," "Follow me," and "Abide in me" are unheeded among many insistent voices. The raucous 'phone proves more demanding than the still small voice of the Spirit. We sadly confess, O Lord, that the home is more pagan than it was fifty years ago. Larger incomes, more comforts, autos, sports, and the growing complexity of life have absorbed our attention, while eternal interests have been eclipsed. We are rebuked by the words, "These ought ye to have done, and not to leave the other undone." Disturb us, O Lord, as we see our blessed homes graduating into mere dormitories and cafeterias. Lead us to better things. May we behold the former blessings coming back. May the pure pleasures and joys of home-life be restored. May our eyes be opened to behold our ever-present Guest, even the precious Lord Jesus. Amen.

GLORIOUS FOURTH

Ye shall know the truth, and the truth shall make you free – John 8:32

We bless Thee for the brave souls who lived through so much grinding history in our land until government became the function of all rather than of a few. We are glad that here and in many lands today, after ages of political tyranny and wrong, the common man has come into his own. Teach us how far we are from reaching any millennial age of perfected politics. Make us aware of such tyrannies of law or labor, of wealth or corporate power, as should be resisted by a spirit of doing justly, loving mercy, and walking humbly with our God. May our ultimate reliance in America not be placed in legislation, knowledge, or material power, but in the character of the average man, knowing that "happy is that nation whose God is the Lord"! Amen.

INDEPENDENCE DAY

Blessed is the nation whose God is Jehovah
— Psalm 33:12

God of our fathers, we remember with grateful hearts those diminutive revolutionary forces in arms against one of the most powerful nations in history. As we recall the course of the Revolutionary conflict, we are constrained to say that Deity was there. We would remember with humility the suffering of a ragged and starving army. We would bless Thy Name that they worked their sure way through cloud and storm and darkness to a victory whose golden values have been increasingly discovered in a century and a half of liberty and democracy, progress and prosperity. "O God, be with us yet, lest we forget, lest we forget!" May we so conduct our personal and national affairs that, fair as is this day, a good age, a grand age, better far than the present, shall follow our generation. In the Name of the Eternal. Amen.

INDEPENDENCE DAY

As free, and not using your freedom for a cloak of wickedness, but as bondservants of God. Honor all men. Love the brotherhood. Fear God —I Peter 2:16, 17

O God of nations, we would humbly and thankfully remember the undaunted courage of our forefathers against the most powerful nation of the Revolutionary period, vindicating at Morristown and Valley Forge, as well as at Saratoga and Yorktown, the ideals of national independence. O God, the foundations were laid in dread, in tears, in partings, in darkness, upon which we now stand in a security which no nation can disturb, glad in the possession of liberties which naught but our own materialism can ever destroy. They sowed in tears; we reap in joy. Now teach us the solemn lesson that if we have no sense of mission matching the moral might of other days, no feeling of responsibility to Thee, we shall share in the common doom of peoples in the past. For the love of country and for the love of Christ, may every one of us contribute to that sum of collective righteousness which alone exalts and preserves a nation. Amen.

LABOR DAY

He that gathereth by labor shall have increase
— Proverbs 13:11

We bless Thee, Thou Creator and ever-living Worker and Upholder of all, that upon one day of the year we are called to consider with gratitude and sympathy the service, the problems, and the welfare of those who are called to lives of physical toil. Help all workers who are discouraged, as they labor under the heat and burden of the day, to remember Jesus Christ. As He once followed the calling of a carpenter may His Figure lend dignity to every honorable occupation. May toilers have the satisfaction of knowing they are adding to the well-being of the world. Guide all organizations of labor to the end that the welfare of the workers of the land may be promoted, co-operation and efficiency in the industrial world secured, and America become increasingly established in righteousness and peace. In the Name of the Carpenter of Nazareth. Amen.

LABOR DAY

Whatsoever ye do, work heartily, as unto the Lord, and not unto men —Colossians 3:23

Heavenly Father, in view of our celebration of Labor Day, make us more thoughtful concerning a better social order. May Christian people earnestly study the bearing of their religion upon social and industrial relations. Give us a profound concern for unemployment in the nation. Help our social engineers to devise ways and means both of eliminating waste from industry and of securing the wisest and most equitable division of its products. Teach us that if we are ever to come to a new and better day, the rich man and the working man and the man on the street must come together in perfect good-will and must contribute their utmost candor, courage and intelligence to the solution of the problem. May the teachings and spirit of Jesus Christ guide us in all things. Amen.

LABOR'S NOBLEMEN

And he said unto them, Extort from no man by violence, neither accuse any one wrongfully; and be content with your wages —Luke 3:14

O Lord, as Labor Day is past and September is here with vacations over, with schools opening, and with a new year of work beginning for many, give us a clearer understanding of the part which physical and mental labor plays in the arrangements of Thy universe. Teach us that humming motors and pounding hammers are all part of the Divine plan and that to each of us is given a piece of work. May we remember that our Master toiled and that He exclaimed also, "My Father worketh." May every man who performs a manly share of work be conscious of his service to Thee, as well as to his fellows. Increase also the number of those who, being warmed and fed by the sweat of other men's brows are humbled by this fact and led to just and generous consideration of working people. In the name of the greatest Workingman of the ages. Amen.

ASH WEDNESDAY

Come ye yourselves apart into a desert place, and rest awhile —Mark 6:31

We thank Thee, O Lord, that the meditative season of the Christian year has come and that incentive is afforded to dwell in grateful and adoring memory upon the virtues and teaching and especially upon the passion and victory of Jesus Christ, Thy Son. May this year's remembrance of the Saviour bring to many of us a sense of the difference between our lives and His. Being rich, He became poor, that He might befriend the forgotten and forlorn. May His life of renunciation be etched over against the things we seek in this indulgent age. Whether or not we fast in the flesh, grant that there may be a stern culture of the soul in these weeks. May we tear off the masks and see our lives as they are and then may we see Jesus living His perfect life and dying His death in utter love for us. Amen.

LENT

As ar as the east is from the west, so far hath he removed our transgressions from us
—Psalm 103:12

Our Heavenly Father, we pray that our lives may be made pure and that we may have a vision of Thee, not as a fleeting glimpse of the Divine but as a daily and hourly peace that passes all understanding. We thank Thee for Jesus, the pure and tender-hearted, the One who was in Himself the express image of Thee, the outshining of Thy glory. Help us to take up His cross and follow in His steps. Deliver us from the stubborness, the uncleanness, the hard-heartedness, the greed, the pride, and the self-will that stand between us and Thee. Give us the spirit of little children who repent quickly, are forgiven often and received always because of their simple trust. If we have been prodigals far from home, help some of us today to say, "I will arise and go unto my father." In the Name of Thy Son. Amen.

LENT

I will be sorry for my sin – Psalm 38:18

O God, in these weeks of directed devotion, we remember with gratitude the lowly birth, the patient home life and the humble toil of our Master. We thank Thee also for His gracious encouragement to the obscure, and His tender forgiveness of the fallen. By all these signs, and yet more by His healing ministry, by the agony in Gethsemane, the brutal cross and the hissing hate of ribald crowds, all of which He bore for us, we know how great was the love wherewith He loved us. And thus, O Lord, however small and insignificant we are in the eyes of men, however ashamed because of false choices, selfish living, or fitful purposes, give us the courage still to say, "I am poor and needy, yet the Lord thinketh on me." In that royal assurance, imbue us with new hope, and remember us in loving kindness. In Jesus' Name. Amen.

LENT

The lust of the flesh and the lust of the eyes and the vain-glory of life, is not of the Father, but is of the world. And the world passeth away, and the lust thereof: but he that doeth the will of God abideth for ever —I John 2:16, 17

We thank Thee, O Lord, for every custom or commandment which causes us to stop and think. Our lives are overfilled with little matters. We often fail to think even of Thee. As we enter upon a period set aside by the Church for meditation, fasting, and prayer, may it mark for many a season when the life is really uncovered to God. May we quiet our passions. May we listen to the higher voices and have the diviner touches fall upon us. Deliver us from any perfunctory keeping of religious rites. If we fast, may it not be irksome but a joy, not a gloomy self-denial, but a gladsome union with our Lord. Save us from any merely transient zeal. May we attain in these forty days a new appreciation of the deeper wisdom and a heavenly goodness. May finer degrees of purity and of charity become a part of us because we have been with Jesus Christ and become partakers of His nature. Amen.

A BETTER LIFE

Show me Thy ways, O Jehovah;
Teach me thy paths
— Psalm 25:4

Heavenly Father, we remember Joseph's purity, Ruth's loyalty, and Amos' courage, and we have seen in some people of today the life we want to live. Help us to follow others so far as they have followed Jesus. We are weak and wavering, but if Thou couldest make fickle Peter into a stedfast martyr, Thou canst also change our cast-iron characters into steel. Make us cautious when temptations come. Give us fortitude for the next trouble. Deliver us from the world's atmosphere and lead us to the spiritual mountaintops where the air is fresh and pure. Teach us to be fair. Increase our faith. Show us where the evil in us lies and give us a wholesome fear of the power of sin. Though weary of our failures, remind us that Thou dost never weary of forgiveness and we may return to Thee freely, without limit. In our Redeemer's Name, and through His Cross. Amen.

CONFESSION

Have mercy, upon me, O God, according to thy loving-kindness;
According to the multitude of thy tender mercies blot out my transgressions — Psalms 51:1

When the best of men, O Lord, lays his life over against the stainless white of Jesus Christ, the "good Paragon of God," he sees the moles and the flaws in his own character. As for most of us, we need only our own consciences to tell us that we have seen and know the better but have chosen the worse. Thou knowest that we have misused our bodies which are temples of the

Holy Spirit. We have given rein to the lust of the flesh, the lust of the eyes, and the pride of life. We have loved the praise of men more than the praise of God. We have been discontented, and even rebellious. We have turned aside from the want and pain of our brethren, "looking every man on his own things rather than the things of others." We have wasted Thy gifts and forgotten Thy love. "Wash us thoroughly from our iniquity and cleanse us from our sin. Purge us with hyssop and we shall be clean. Wash us thoroughly and we shall be whiter than snow." And when we have heard the gracious Voice of forgiveness, "Neither do I condemn thee," may we heed that same Voice when we are told, "Go, and sin no more." In Jesus' Name. Amen.

FOLLOWING CHRIST

Believe thou in me – John 14:1
Learn of me – Matthew 11:29
Follow me – Luke 9:59

Heavenly Father, bless every believer in Jesus Christ who follows Him in thought through these weeks from the cradle to the cross and sepulcher and unto Mt. Olivet. We would inwardly walk and talk with Him even though our days are full of absorbing tasks. We would keep our tryst with Him in Thy fear and truth and joy. Help us to consecrate some definite portion of our time to quietness and meditation or to public worship. Help us to make some special inquiry into the meaning of Jesus' teaching or friendship or example or holy cross. Help us to think more gently of our brother man. Help us not to squander these days of spiritual opportunity in the usual passion for accumulation or pleasure but to harvest them for the great things of the soul. In the Name of our Lord and Master. Amen.

FOSSIL HEARTS

And I will give them one heart, and I will put a new spirit within you; and I will take the stony heart out of their flesh, and will give them a heart of flesh —Ezekiel 11:19

We thank Thee for childhood's purity, love, and prayerfulness. We bless Thee that under the nurture of Christian homes there may be projected into youth and later years the same tenderness, freshness, and faith. Alas, O Lord, that we should ever lose our religious fervor of heart! And yet we confess that many of us have succumbed to the hardening influences of life, and have become almost as cold and rigid as marble. We respond but faintly to the higher world. Spiritual faculties are blunted. The fine thrills of youthful idealism have been replaced by the scoffs of the world. O God, have pity upon us and work a miracle within us. Help the young to keep their hearts single, simple, and sincere. If the subtle chemistry of nature has changed the capacity for large feelings and rich visions into the dullness of stone, may the omnipotent grace of Christ take the stony hearts out of us and give us hearts of flesh. In Jesus' Name. Amen.

MODERN DEMASES

Demas forsook me — II Timothy 4:10

We confess, O Lord, in this Lenten season that many of us have set our hands to the plow and turned back. In early life we have had our dream, we have seen the "vision splendid," and we have begun the journey toward the Celestial City, only later to desert. We have started merrily but have dragged wearily and quit shamefully. We have been full of good resolutions which we did not keep. We have escaped from evil companions and hurtful habits only to return to them. Our faces once shone with the fervor of our first love of goodness. Now they are dull. We have been constant in nothing but our inconstancy. But we thank Thee that we need not despair. If we own our fault there is One at our side to help. Among the faithless Thou wast ever faithful. Thou didst set Thy face steadfastly toward Calvary. Thou dost offer us Thy pardon and Thy fortitude. "All things are possible to him that believeth." "Lord, I believe. Help thou my unbelief." Amen.

THE CHARITY OF LINCOLN

Love suffereth long, and is kind, . . . seeketh not its own, is not provoked, taketh not account of evil, beareth all things. . . . Love never faileth –I Corinthians 13:4-8

O God of love, give us that charity that "suffereth long and is kind." In the midst of so much that is bitter and vindictive in this world, we would have the patience, the poise, and the forgiving love which Abraham Lincoln had, and which he learned from Jesus Christ. We are glad that, when the great Emancipator "was reviled, he reviled not. Again, when he suffered, he threatened not." We thank Thee for his serenity under circumstances which might have justified resentment. As America thinks of this great, magnanimous soul, so free from rancor, jealousy, or prejudice, may thousands of her sons and daughters be led to cultivate a spirit of good-will. Deliver us from the vice of vindictiveness, and, with minds forgetful of past offenses, give us sincere thoughts and a heart to love our brethren. In the Name of the Son of Man. Amen.

LINCOLN, THE SERVANT OF ALL

Ye know that the rulers of the Gentiles . . . exercise authority over them. Not so shall it be among you. . . whosoever would become great among you shall be your minister; and whosoever would be first among you shall be your servant —Matthew 20:25, 26, 27

O God of our Fathers, we are grateful that although our national history includes but a period of a century and a half, yet our "cloud of witnesses" is gathering in the skies which will inspire us even as Israel's men of faith, canonized in the book of Hebrews, led Paul and Peter, James and John. O Lord, we bless Thee today for Abraham Lincoln, who, of all our patriot saints, seems most nearly to fulfill the outlines of the life of the Nazarene. We wonder how often the glow of the pine knots lighted that sacred page where it is written "The Son of man came not to be ministered unto, but to minister." We thank Thee that he believed the service of humanity to be the ultimate moral reality in the Kingdom of God. Help us to remember that before he made the involuntary sacrifice of his life, he had already passed through veritable Gethsemanes and Calvarys for his country, evincing his deliberate philosophy of service and sacrifice. May his memory never cease to inspire likemindedness in us and in the future generations. In Jesus' Name. Amen.

MEMORIAL DAY

This . . . shall be spoken of for a memorial
— Mark 14:9

O God of America and of all nations, may we pause for a day to think of our debt to the past. We know that if the vast invisible choir made up of our ancestors were able to speak, we should learn that from one come our strength of body, from another our energy of will, from another our accuracy of judgment and from another our faith in the Unseen. May we be grateful to the generations that taught us the love of beauty so that music, painting and poetry have become a part of daily life. May we remember the pioneers whose adventure was incredible and whose toil was untold. May we bless Thee for Jefferson, Hamilton and Madison whose political thinking laid the foundations of the republic. May we never forget the heroes of our wars who secured our original freedom, who preserved our integrity, and who helped other nations in their extremity. We would revere the yesterdays of the race. We would bless Thee for our patriots. We would pray Thee that the past might be an inspiration to rectitude and service in the future. In Jesus' Name. Amen.

MEMORIAL DAY

The righteous shall be had in everlasting remembrance —Psalm 112:6

O God of our Fathers, may Memorial Day arouse in us the instinct of patriotism by its suggestions of past history, illustrious characters, and immortal heroisms. Life seems great and imperishable, as, over against so much that is mean and base in the world of today, stands out the white background of the great and generous devotion of the past. If there are stains upon the life of the community or the state which tend to depress us, may we make some allowance for those imperfections which are never absent from organized society. May we remember that in the country as a whole, there are many who are giving fortune and life for the public good with an unhesitating cheerfulness, and that out of this period of unheroic moods and pursuits legions of the loyal would die for the country, as their fathers did, were we confronted by a sudden crisis. Show us how to conduct ourselves in this material age so that we shall not lose the great realities of duty and sacrifice, but be able to hand to the next generation the torch of freedom, as the past generation has entrusted it to us. In the Name of Christ. Amen.

MEMORIAL DAY

Who through faith subdued kingdoms, wrought righteousness, . . . from weakness were made strong, waxed mighty in war

—Hebrews 11:33, 34

O God of this Christian nation, we would remember days that are gone and lives that were spent in a noble cause. We have strewn upon hallowed ground not ashes that betoken desolation and despair, but flowers emblematic of living beauty and undying love. The hillocks which mark the last resting-places of our honored soldier-dead eloquently speak to the living of today concerning the chivalry of yesterday. As we think of them may our hearts pulsate anew with soul-stirring thoughts of our native land. We know that they and all unselfish servants of society will have died in vain if ever a generation appears which does not furnish its quota of the unblemished and loyal who will not shirk the posts of public service for private reasons of cowardice or selfishness. God, grant that the patriotism of the past, so precious and pure, may be matched by a similar patriotism of the present and future. God, bless our native land! Amen.

THE MIDDLE STATE

The years draw nigh, when thou shalt say, I have no pelasure in them —Ecclesiastes 12:1

Lord Jesus, Thou who art Alpha and Omega, we would recall the gracious promise, "Lo, I am with you always." We are conscious of the middle years, and sometimes lament, "Where is the blessedness which once I knew when first I saw the Lord?" Many of us feed our safety deposit boxes and starve our souls; and we are growing hard. We worship deeds and facts and cash. We beseech Thee to have mercy upon us so that in our forties and fifties we shall be as trees that have weathered the storms and still bring forth fruit in their season. May we so abide in the ever living Vine that we may bear the graces of the Holy Spirit which are love, joy, and peace. Amen.

THE TEMPTATIONS OF MIDDLE-LIFE

O Jehovah, revive thy work in the midst of the years;
In the midst of the years make it known

—Habakkuk 3:2

O God of all goodness and power, we who are in our forties and fifties come to Thee to make our confession and implore Thy grace for our time of need. The world has been trying to make us like itself. It has despoiled us of our dreams. Its unbelief has pervaded our souls. We have been content with a little idealism and an occasional touch with the Divine, while success and costly pleasures have absorbed our interest. We have wanted to be great not in the thing itself, but with a greatness that men could see. The strong inner voices of our earlier years are almost stilled. But now we would return to Thee. "We would see Jesus." May the Holy Spirit reveal to us His all-engaging character. May the winsomeness of His love, the poise of His humility, the perfection of His manhood, and the salvation of His Cross restore our souls and lead us in the paths of righteousness for His Name's sake. Amen.

THE TESTS OF MIDDLE-LIFE

I have fought the good fight, I have finished the course, I have kept the faith –II Timothy 4:7

Our Heavenly Father, help those of us who are in our late forties, our fifties, or our sixties to keep a stout heart, a clear faith, and an undiscourageable patience amid the disappointments, the burdens, the sorrows, and the financial cares that come to us in this period of our lives. May we remember the words of the great Apostle who said, "I have finished the course," and grant that at the end of our lives, also, we may not have to look back upon a good beginning spoiled by a poor ending. Save us from the moral collapses that so often overtake those who are bearing the heat and burden of the day. When the circumstances of our lives tend to provoke us to bitterness or impatience, to covetousness, materialism, and the misuse of power, do Thou draw near to correct, to suggest, to comfort, or to control and let us feel Thee near us as we did in youth. As we face the inescapable facts of maturity, keep us sweet and pure, calm and unafraid, and may we enter upon our old age as worthy as when we turned our twenties. In the Name of Him who on the cross could cry, "It is finished!" Amen.

MOTHER'S DAY

Can a woman forget her sucking child?
—Isaiah 49:15

O Lord, we are thinking of our mothers today. What they meant to us we can never fully know. When our little hearts were lonely, we laid them against mother's heart which beat with our own. O God, how we bless Thee for these nurturing, forgiving, loving mothers of ours! Let us render them now the homage of grateful hearts and let us exert our sincerest effort for the girls of today who are to be the mothers of tomorrow. May we resist all influences, institutions, and customs – all pictures, books, and amusements which would destroy the perennial sanctity and ministry of motherhood. In all we do and say and are, may we heed the sacred injunction, "Honor thy mother!" In the Name of the Son of Mary. Amen.

MOTHER'S DAY

The unfeigned faith that is in thee . . . dwelt first in thy . . . mother —II Timothy 1:5

O God, we thank Thee for the love of our mothers. When we were sick, it chased sleep from their eyes through the watchful night. When we were in trouble, it kissed our tears away. When we erred, its "gentleness made us great." Yea, we thank Thee, O Lord, for the sweet passion of our mothers. It has bidden our ambitions rise. It has bettered whatever in us was best. It has taught us a wholesome shame of the sordid and base. If we have learned any of the sweet civilities of life, we know how much we owe to the refined mind of our mothers. God bless them today wherever they are. If redeemed above, help us, having the love of them in our hearts, to purify ourselves of all dross even as they are pure. If they are spared to us here below, may a new spirit of love, quick and fresh, spring up within us, that we may yield them the utmost of duty and adoration. In th Name of Mary's Son. Amen.

OUR MOTHERS

My son, hear the instruction of thy father,
And forsake not the law of thy mother

—Proverbs 1:8

Heavenly Father, we can believe in Thee more easily because Thou didst ever make a mother. We thank Thee for the loving care, the radiant presence, the spiritual light, the unvarying truthfulness, and the unceasing vigilance of our dear mothers. We wonder, O Lord, whether their ministries cease when they are taken to heaven. May we indulge the faith that mysterious longings after holiness, intense desires for purity that drives away sordid thought, comforts, helps, graces that do not seem to originate within our own selves, have descended like showers upon us as answers to the prayers of our beloved before the Throne. Grant that every man and woman, every boy and girl who enjoy mother-love here and now, may rightly value this treasure, may so live that her travail and tears may not be in vain and may fill her days with those evidences of affection which are sweeter to her "than honey and the honeycomb." In Jesus' Name. Amen.

THE COMMONWEALTH OF FAITH

For one is your Master, even Christ; and all ye are brethren —Matthew 23:8.

Help us, O Lord, to love our brother man in every clime. Deliver America from the sin of national vainglory. Rid us of a superior attitude to other nations or individuals. Forgive us if we have come to think of ourselves as favorites of Heaven. Impress upon us the teachings and example of Jesus until we catch His conception of the great human family — the great brotherhood of man. May we have faith in each other, and try to discover the broad basis of worth in every man whatever his color, creed, or nationality. Make the democracy of Jesus triumphant everywhere. May every valley where other people have overcome the centuries be exalted. May every mountain of pride and greed be laid low. May the day hasten when no nation will live to itself, but all will live for the great brotherhood and when, having loved men whom we have seen, we shall come to love God whom we have not seen. In the Name of Him who gave Himself that all might be one in Him. Amen.

ELECTION DAY

I defy the armies of Israel this day; give me a man, that we may fight together —I Samuel 17:10

We give praise to Thee, O God, that we live in a day when the divine right of kings, after thousands of years of supremacy, has become obsolete. We thank Thee that all over this world great democracies are found where men feel the touch and inspiration of the free air that blows over mountains and plains, and look to themselves as the immediate agents of the divine will in bringing about a better life for mankind. May the time never come when by our own apathy and neglect we lose our power of self-determination. Help us, while recognizing the necessity of parties in a free government, to put conscience into our political action. In all elections may we learn how to discriminate between party loyalty and that enlightened independent action without which our government must inevitably be handed over to the forces of corruption and misrule. May Thy Kingdom come and Thy will be done on earth as it is done in heaven. Amen.

ELECTION DAY

Look ye out the best and meetest of your master's sons, and set him on his father's throne, and fight for your master's house —II Kings 10:3

O God of nations, make every voter in America aware of the high privilege which is his of going to the ballot-box and helping to settle the issues of his country. May we remember how men have wrought and suffered and died that the voice of the strong might be no mightier than the voice of the weak. And, as this is the medium through which we act upon our country, help us to vote with a sense of solemn responsibility. Give us a chief magistrate who shall take hold of the government with clean, strong, and patriotic hands. When the emotions of the hour have subsided, may the calm level of public opinion below the storm bear upon its bosom the proud ship of state sailing on an even keel, under bright skies, pointed to a sure haven, and under a commander chosen and anointed by the Most High. Amen.

FOR THE PRESIDENT-ELECT

Thou rulest over all; and in thy hand is power and might; and in thy hand it is to make great, and to give strength unto all —I Chronicles 29:12

As another election has come and gone, help us, O Lord, to remember that Thou dost rule the destinies of nations. Thou dost exalt one; thou dost humble another. Yet we bless Thee that Thou art not a capricious Ruler, but One who meteth out justice and righteousness to all peoples. May the American nation so walk before Thee in law and order, in equity and unity, in peace and good-will, that it may continue to receive Thy favor. Guide our lawmakers that they may lead us in the ways of wisdom, goodness and truth. Especially bless the President-elect that his administration may promote righteous government in all our domestic and foreign relations. In Christ's Name. Amen.

OUR NEW PRESIDENT

Fear thou not, for I am with thee; be not dismayed, for I am thy God; I will strengthen thee; yea, I will help thee; yea, I will uphold thee with the right hand of my righteousness —Isaiah 41:10

We bless Thee, Thou God of nations, for our beloved, enchanted land. We thank Thee that with visions of such a land men struggled forward for ages, and though dungeon dreams and fagot flames marked many generations, the heavens opened and the vision brightened. And now we are rejoicing in the great day of the Lord! The people have come to power! Help us to receive and use our blessing in the spirit of wonder and humility. What are freedom and power without virtue but injustice and wrong? May our supreme good never become an infinite curse! Give to our new leader a profound, tender, and holy respect for the country's power which he holds in his hand today. May he so guide this Republic in the fear of God that toil shall have its wage, that justice shall be supreme, and that honor shall be revered. So gird and endow him that his administration shall build our walls in righteousness and establish our gates in peace. In Jesus' Name. Amen.

NATIONAL RIGHTEOUSNESS

God is our refuge and strength,
A very present help in trouble.

—Psalm 46:1

We look to Thee, O Jehovah of hosts, to bare Thine arm and save America for human freedom as Thou didst save Israel. Thou knowest that the very survival of this nation beyond the present century is involved in the power being applied both openly and in subtle intrigue by a mighty foe and an enemy even of Thyself as Ruler of nations. Shall Russia gain the sovereignty of this entire hemisphere and bury America? If the light of freedom is not to die, if the character of human society is not to be warped into a pagan image, O Lord, we pray Thee to deal with this atheistic affront to Thy Being as Thou hast ever dealt with the "nations that forget God." May we not depend too long on the reservoir of spiritual strength which was stored by our forefathers. May America set its face like a flint against over-weening luxury, economic greed, sex mania, crime, and drink. May we repent of our national sins and prove more worthy of Thy divine forgiveness and help. In Jehovah's Name. Amen.

LAW AND ORDER

For Jehovah hath a controversy with the inhabitants of the land, because there is no truth, nor goodness, nor knowledge of God in the land. [By] swearing, and breaking faith, and killing, and stealing, and committing adultery; they break out, and blood toucheth, blood

—Hosea 4:1, 2

Remembering, O Lord, that ours is a Christian nation, we would unite with all who understand our present moral situation in a cry to Thee for heavenly succor. We lament the breakdown of self-restraint, the wild careers with reins thrown upon the neck of willful desire, the cities ruled by lawless elements, a nation shamed by its record of crime. Arrest the forces of organized greed. Humble us to perceive the truth that it is not merely by the agency of the courts or the expedient of a mechanical self-discipline that we can meet our situation, but by a cleansing and inspiration that can come only from Thee, for it is "not by might, nor by power, but by my Spirit, saith the Lord of Hosts." Therefore, establish Thy reign in our hearts and we shall render unto Caesar that which is Caesar's and unto God that which is God's. In the Name of Christ. Amen.

OUR NATION AND GOD

The kingdom is Jehovah's;
And he is the ruler over the nations

—Psalm 22:28

O Thou, who art our father's God and our God, we would humble ourselves and repent of our national sins. May we not be smug and complacent when the very wolves are howling in the woods about us, and fierce blasts of snow and ice are bursting against our fancied security. May we not pave a path of safety with coins that state, "In God we trust!" May we bring forth fruits meet for repentance. Give us a piercing sense of guilt as we see so many of our children going astray, our Sabbath Day disappearing, crime increasing, liquor winning, luxury growing, humanitarianism decreasing, unity threatened, and suicidal war a possibility. God, make the Church through a revival of true religion the agent of the necessary regeneration in American life, which alone can save our nation. In Jehovah's Name. Amen.

GOD AND WORLD WAR

Who coverest thyself with light as with a garment;
Who stretchest out the heavens like a curtain;
Who layeth the beams of his chambers in the waters;
Who maketh the clouds his chariot;
Who walketh up on the wings of the wind

—Psalm 104:2, 3

O God, the Ruler of all, may there be "a sound of going in the tops of the mulberry trees" as "God moves in a mysterious way His wonders to perform." Let Thy voice be heard above the world's storms, commanding, "Peace, be still!" Let the mountains of hate be flattened to earth and let the peaks of moderation, decency, and understanding be lifted up. Let the floods of the wicked threatening the destruction of many peoples be transformed into rivers of gold wherewith the hungry millions of the world may be fed. As for those who abhor Thee, destroy their fruit from above and their roots from beneath. O Jehovah of Hosts, bring sudden destruction upon the strong who cast down righteousness and turn justice into wormwood. Instead of confusion and dismay throughout the world, let judgment roll down as waters and righteousness as a mighty stream. May no weapon that is formed against Thee prosper, and may every tongue that shall rise against Thee in judgment be condemned. Thus may "thy kingdom come and thy will be done in earth as it is in heaven." Amen.

THE NEW YEAR

I shall go softly all my years —Isaiah 38:15

Our heavenly Father, we thank Thee for sunshine after rain, for bright mornings after dark nights, for new years after old. Thy goodness is as limitless as space or time. Our hearts are glad as we realize that although we cannot correct mistakes we have made in the past year, or cut out unworthy pages written in indelible ink, yet, so far as Thine attitude toward us is concerned, we can take courage, remembering how Thou hast said, "I have blotted out thy transgressions, and will remember no more thy sins." And now, O Lord, as Thou hast set before us an open door, a new year, a clean page, this is our prayer: may our minds and bodies be kept pure, our homes sacred, our hearts brave, and our spirits right. May Jesus be our example and the Bible our guide. May God be our Partner and the Holy Spirit our Comforter. Around our hearthstones make us a blessing. May we be a wholesome influence in our social life. May we be found frequently in our Father's house. In Jesus' Name. Amen.

A HAPPY NEW YEAR

If they hearken and serve him,
They shall spend their days in prosperity,
And their years in pleasures

—Job 36:11

O Lord, as we step now into the path of another year, our hearts are humbled to think how unworthy we are of Thy patience with us. In our best moments we acknowledge Thee to be the Lord and we know there is no other life worth living but the good life. Deliver us from the sights that dazzle and from the fever of desire. Create within us clean hearts and renew a right spirit. May the New Year be a happy one because we shall live lives that are strong and true and clean, and because we shall walk hand in hand with Thee. Make our bodies strong for the burdens we must bear. Make our consciences true as a magnet to the pole. Even should we be beset with cares or required to drink the cup of sorrow in a night of weeping, still may the day dawn and the shadows flee away before the brightness of Thy presence. May there be innocent and satisfying mirth and music in our lives because the joy of the Lord is in our hearts. In Jesus' Name. Amen.

THE DAYS OF OUR YEARS

I, Jehovah thy God, will hold thy right hand,
saying unto thee, Fear not; I will help thee

—Isaiah 41:13

Father in Heaven, may we remember that all the blessings which have been handed to us in such profusion during the year just closed have come from thy generous hand. Make us more sensitive to Thee, more appreciative of Thine unwearying ministry from generation to generation. Our hearts are glad as we realize that, although we cannot correct mistakes we have made in the past year or cut out unworthy pages written in indelible ink – yet, so far as Thine attitude toward us is concerned, we can take courage, remembering how Thou hast said, "I have blotted out thy transgressions and will remember no more thy sins." Forgive not only our ingratitude but also all our shortcomings. Forgive suspicions, sinful imaginations, prayerless and powerless lives. May a great upward surge of desire for a worthier existence possess us. As the New Year opens, may it find us soberly but not morbidly surveying the past, thoughtfully reflecting upon Thy undeserved and unlimited mercy, and trustfully taking Thy hand to walk in the coming days more closely with Thee than we have ever done before. In Jesus' Name. Amen.

GRATITUDE FOR ANOTHER YEAR

Lord, Thou hast been our dwelling-place
In all generations

–Psalm 90:1

O Lord, we are grateful for the providence which has already assured us in the opening days of the New Year that Thou art still patient with us. Thou hast forgiven us seventy times seven. How we hurry and worry one another, but Thou dost not hurry us. A thousand years in Thy sight are but a day. Thou dost wait for humanity to come around to Thy ways and Thy thoughts. Shame us by this Thy divine forbearance. May we leave off our mistakes and trying out of foolish and vain ideas and sit at the feet of the One who said, "Learn of me." O Master-Craftsman, watch, guide, direct us in the holy art of life as through another year we strive to become workmen "that need not to be ashamed." Amen.

THE OLD YEAR

I have blotted out, as a thick cloud, thy transgressions, and, as a cloud, thy sins; return unto me; for I have redeemed thee –Isaiah 44:22

It is with humble hearts, O Lord, that we approach the end of another year. We are afraid that we are no better men and women than we were at the beginning of the year. Too often, instead of the fruits of love, joy, and peace, our hearts have borne bitterness, malice, or the poison of gross desire. Forgive us for our falsehood, our envy, and our irreverence. Forgive our easygoing way of expecting that some time, some way, we shall outgrow our infirmities, when all the while, for lack of serious attention to our case, we are weakening in our moral fiber and waiting for a tomorrow that will never come. Save us, however, from despair. In Jesus' Name. Amen.

PEACE

And he will judge between the nations, and will decide concerning many peoples; and they shall beat their swords into plowshares, and their spears into pruning-hooks; nation shall not lift up sword against nation, neither shall they learn war any more – Isaiah 2:3, 4

O Lord, bring in the knowledge of Thee as our Father and of every man as our brother. May war upon black wings fly to the uttermost part of the sea to be known no more. May eternal peace be established as a spirit and be embodied in suitable institutions and agreements between nations. May the lion and the lamb lie down together. Give us all the grace to see the folly, the horror, and the menace involved in another armed conflict in Christendom. Help us to substitute reason for force, trust for suspicion, the open palm of brotherhood for the mailed fist of enmity, the spirit of charity and forgiveness which Thou dost exemplify for Satan's spirit of hatred and vindictive fury. And when the Day of the Lord shall come, the glory shall be to Thy Name, Father, Son, and Holy Spirit. Amen.

PEACE ON EARTH

Seek peace, and pursue it –Psalm 34:14

Deliver us, O Lord, from the complacency of the Pharisee. Show to us and to all other nations that if the peoples of the earth magnify their own virtues and minimize their shortcomings, they set up a barrier between themselves and those who should be their friends. Remind us that if we look upon neighbor nations with grudging or only partial acknowledgment of their worthy achievements and a resentful exaggeration of their faults, we are cultivating the spirit that leads to war. Give us the charity and the tactical wisdom of Jesus who counseled and practiced overcoming evil with good. May we begin the peace movement in our own hearts. Grant unto us a spirit of brotherhood that knows no dividing lines because of the common Fatherhood which we share. In Jesus' Name. Amen.

WORLD PEACE

How beautiful upon the mountains are the feet of him that bringeth good tidings, that publisheth peace – Isaiah 52:7

Eternal God, immortal Love, we thank Thee that the statesmen of all lands are consecrating their best energies to making the world a brotherhood. May the masses upon whom war's burdens have always fallen most heavily create a solid body of public opinion that shall save international agreements from becoming forgotten documents in the archives of the nations. May the common people demand sincerity and consistency with the ideal that nation shall not rise up against nation for any purpose whatever. May America be a nation of informed citizens concerning this most unbelievable step. May the people rise in their might to demand that the present course of the United States not to go to war independently unless we are attacked shall remain inviolate. In Christ's Name. Amen.

THE CONSEQUENCES OF SIN

The wages of sin is death; but the free gift of God is eternal life in Christ Jesus our Lord

—Romans 6:23

How many of us, O Lord, have learned that "whatsoever a man soweth that shall he also reap." We know the folly of vice. The results of dishonesty, impurity, intemperance, hatred, and greed have made deep scars in our souls. Even Thy forgiveness does not remove the bitter past or the blighting present. Yet our hearts take courage as we know that we are always welcome to return to Thee. Thou art the eternal Father of the prodigal. We may start afresh and be loved and regarded as though nothing had happened. A new life may begin within us which fights the consequences of the old. Broken relations can be repaired, old debts paid, and old wrongs righted. We bless Thee that Thou dost repair the waste places in our souls. May the law of changeless love begin to operate in some wretched man today and overcome the law of sin and death. In Jesus' Name. Amen.

THE FICTIONS OF SIN

The way of a fool is right in his own eyes;
But he that is wise hearkeneth unto counsel
—Proverbs 12:15

We thank Thee, O Lord, for the candor of Thy Word. The inspired record never softens the facts of human sin. We thank Thee for the sure warning which comes down to us from the truthful portraits of the Bible. Make us genuine. As we advance in culture and use milder words for less pleasant terms, may this glossing over of plain names and hard facts not be carried into our moral life. May stubbornness and stinginess and lying and lust not lose their repellent character by being dressed up in better language. If cruelty, avarice, pride, or evil desire is really ruling us, give us the understanding to see our sin. With sincere sorrow may we repent and seek the forgiveness of God through our faith in Jesus Christ. Amen.

THE SINS OF THE SAINTS

If a man say, I love God, and hateth his brother, he is a liar: for he that loveth not his brother whom he hath seen, cannot love God, whom he hath not seen —I John 4:20

Help us, O Lord, to remember the words of Jesus, how He said, "Cast the beam out of thine own eye." May we who claim to live lives of integrity and who are enrolled in the Church realize that respectable professions and even religious faith do not guarantee all the virtues. If the effort to be just has made us also hard, if our honesty has not been associated with tenderness, if our zeal for the truth has made us narrow, help us to realize that these failings may hurt the cause of Christ more than our loyalty to Him may help it. Some of us are bitter and hard. Some of us are dishonorable. Some of us are unforgiving. Some are untruthful. O Lord, help all who name Thy Name to depart from every form of iniquity, to lay aside every weight and the sin that doth so easily beset us. In Jesus' Name. Amen.

†

SPRING

All things work together for good —Romans 8:28

We bless Thee, Giver of tongues to praise, that the cold heart of the weary Winter has stirred and warmed and softened into the mildness of Spring. Our love goes forth to meet the lovely time. Behold, "all things work together for good." With divine deftness Thou art working in bulb and bush and bud. The tiny leaf of brushwood and elm is fresh from Thy touch. The moist rich smell of the earth, the tulip's cheek painted with many carats of gold, the vale, vocal with the joy of arriving birds, springing plants, growing trees, fields breathing sweetly, young lovers meeting, are all but the opening of the heart of God. Therefore we avow again our love to Thee. Thou art good beyond all words to utter. Blessed be Thy Name forever and ever. Amen.

†

SPRING

For lo, the winter is past;
The flowers appear on the earth;
The time of the singing of birds is come,
And the voice of the turtle-dove is heard in our land —Song of Solomon 2:11, 12

O God, we thank Thee for the world Thou hast given us for a home. It is a very beautiful world in these days of advancing Spring. All nature seems like a glorious symphony or a sacrament of beauty. We bless Thee for the sweetness of flowers, the joy and promise of the morning sun, for frozen buds that have burst into blossoms, for the throats of birds flooded with new songs, for the rich embroidery of sunlight traced upon the delicate green of the elms. We thank Thee for the early promise of roses and butterflies, golden fields of wheat, and marching ranks of corn. Truly it is a second New Year! Help us in these kindly days to forget the winter and frost, and the bitter winds. As we consider the lilies of the fields, may our spirits quit their tombs and walk with Thee in the garden in all the glad hopefulness of Spring. Amen.

SPRING

The Mighty One, God, Jehovah, hath spoken,
And called the earth from the rising of the sun
unto the going down thereof.
Out of Zion, the perfection of beauty,
God hath shined forth

—Psalm 50:1, 2

Maker of men and Lord of all existence, at the Springtime hour, we turn to Thee, to adore and praise Thee for the unveiling of Thyself in the power, beauty, and beneficence of great Nature about us. Especially do we praise Thee for the gracious glimpse of the tenderness and warmth of Thy Being which is vouchsafed us as the leaves and the grass come forth, as the crocus, the dandelion and the violet appear, and as the happy birds return. The green traceries of the elms, like a thousand smiles of Thine, and the soft breezes make us feel that Thy love is pervading all the earth. "Thou deckest thyself with light as with a garment." Whatever we see and wherever we go, we are reminded of Thee. We are constrained to feel that even with all Nature's happy message in the colorful days of early Spring, the half has not been told us of the gentleness of God which passes knowledge. In the Name of Him who said, "Consider the lilies of the field." Amen.

BLESSED SPRING

I went down into the garden of nuts,
To see the green plants of the valley,
To see whether the vine budded,
And the pomegranates were in flower
—Song of Solomon 6:11

Holy Lord, "all Thy works shall praise Thy name in earth and sea and sky!" Thy presence grows real to us in the beauty of the world Thou hast made. Sometimes when we turn within, life loses some of its dignity and loveliness, but when we consider the heavens which Thou hast made, when gladness flowers up from the blossoming ground, when the song of the bird and the hum of the bee come to us on the fragrant air and the cooling breeze, then we know it is no time to be sad or cloudy, cynical or glum. Only Thou, O Lord, couldest make such a world as this, and, as it reflects the light and love of Thy countenance, so does our ability to respond to its meanings betray our kinship to Thee. Thou art very good, and all that is good in us is from Thee, and is a part of Thee. Sanctify us more and more into Thy likeness as we break the bread of heaven and drink the dew of the morning in Nature's sacrament of beauty. Amen.

†

APRIL

Thou renewest the face of the ground
—Psalm 104:30

In the Springtime, O Lord, Thou dost put a new song in our mouths. Behold the hills are radiant and fair. Now leaping grass springs in the meadows. Thou dost walk down the dales and spread a carpet soft and green, and worked with lovely flowers. Joyous birds flit happily in the branches of the trees and pour their praises into a divine symphony. Sparkling dews, budding flower-cups, gracious showers – how they fill us with surprising joy, and how sure they make us that Thou art the Creator of the world! O Divine Renewer of the earth, we thank Thee for the new-born glow of faith, for the rapture of glad new songs, and most of all, for "Thyself, best Gift Divine." As Thou hast given us eyes to see and hearts to feel in the mellow atmosphere of these Spring days, so help us also to find and read Thee everywhere in Thy world. In Jesus' Name. Amen.

MAY

The flowers appear on the earth;
The time of the singing of birds is come
—Song of Solomon 2:12

Make us, O Lord, to be lovers of the meadows and of the woods so that we shall be lovers of Thee. Forbid that we should permit "the cares of the world, the pleasures of this life, or the deceitfulness of riches" to rob us of the delight in the continual symphony of color which we may enjoy now for three quarters of the year. How can we close our hearts to Nature's great brotherhood as it breaks into a thousand smiles in May and laughes a golden harvest in summer? Father of all goodness, Causer of pleasure and light, truly Thy love pervades the earth. Thou art not only the Maker of men, but the Fashioner of flowers, the Distiller of dew, the Creator of fruitful trees, the Inspirer of the songs of birds. Thou makest the outgoings of the morning and evening to praise Thee. "O tender God! if Thou art so loving in Thy creatures, how fair and lovely must Thou be in Thyself!" We would glorify and enjoy Thee forever. Amen.

MAYTIME

How the leaves and the grass come forth; how the beautiful flowers smile; how the forest and the heath and the meadows resound with the sweet songs of the nightingale and other small birds; how humanity, young and old, manifest their joy in merry and gladsome utterances

—From the German mystic Suso

Lord, we look across the fields and see the beauty of May and we realize anew that "Thou deckest Thyself with light as with a garment." Give us eyes to see and ears to hear, that we may catch more than the perfume of the blossoms and see more than the flower-tinted meadows. The perfume comes not from the air, but from Thee. The pattern of Spring's lovely landscape proclaims to us that the beauty of the Lord our God is upon the face of the land. We thank Thee for all the fair sights of this season. How profuse are the flowers – some standing in grouped gladness pouring forth their choral ecstasies to Thee; some sitting apart but singing a quiet and lovely song, but all uniting in the May festival of praises. Truly, O God, Thou livest and breathest through all things. May our glory awake! May we join the chorus of Spring! Give "beauty for ashes, the oil of joy for mourning, the garment of praise for the spirit of heaviness." Amen.

GOD'S SMILE IN NATURE

The heavens declare the glory of God;
And the firmament showeth his handiwork.
Day unto day uttereth speech,
And night unto night showeth knowledge
—Psalm 19:1, 2

O God, we thank Thee that in the orderly procession of the seasons Spring has come again in the fullness of her beauty. Thou hast dressed field and wood with lovely tinted robes of green, hast scented them with magic odors, and hast put a new song into the mouths of a thousand birds. We are glad that when we lift our eyes out in the great open at night we behold not a curtain of inky black, but the "spangled heavens, a shining frame." We feel calm when we know the stars are shining. They seem to ray forth the endless patience and infinite kindness of the Divine. We thank Thee for all Thy beauty in the heavens and the earth. We bless Thee for "the pomp of morning, the glory of noon, and the splendor of the sunset." May we believe, and find our everlasting peace through Him, even Jesus, "who also made the worlds." Amen.

SUMMERTIME

Consider the lilies of the field —Matthew 6:28

We love to think, Holy Father, Lover of Beauty, that "Thou hast made the summer." Azure skies, green hill-sides, golden fields, "soft airs and song and light and bloom" — all these come from Thee, the great Giver of all good. May Nature ever act for us in a truly sacramental way. May its power, order, and beauty tell part of the story of the Divine heart. May even the irreverent and faithless not miss its meaning. Though they may never know the rapture of the mystic whose faith sees beyond the near and the evident, yet when nature dresses all the landscape with shimmering robes of green and scents it with magic odors, may thoughts of Thee be stirred instinctively in their breasts. Though at the end of this season some may have cause again to say, "The harvest is past, the summer is ended, and we are not saved," may more discern in the Summer a vesture only partly concealing His glory, a sacrament of eternal truth, and may they seek His ways and live. In the Name of Jesus Christ. Amen.

†

DOG DAYS

Now the Lord of peace himself give you peace at all times in all ways

—II Thessalonians 3:16

O God, give us strength and coolness and balm in the oppressive days of August. Weeks of work wear our bodies and souls. The ruts appear in our path. We become habit-bound in ordinary thinking and commonplace behavior. We are thankful for the courage and strength to remain at the post of duty, but forbid, Lord, that we should be entangled in the mesh of physical things which try to do their worst with us in the heat of Summer. Deliver us from all seasonal temptations. If we are weary may we be grateful that it is honorable to be "weary in well-doing." Make us contented in industry, thankful for health, and thankful that we can earn a living. Along our hot and dusty pathway, cause a well of spiritual water to gush out, lead us to the shadow of a rock in a weary land, and show us yet once again that, in season and out of season, Thou art watching over us in a loving and provident Fatherhood. In Jesus' Name. Amen.

THE BREATH OF THE CREATOR

And Jehovah God formed man of the dust of the ground, and breathed into his nostrils the breath of life —Genesis 2:7

Father of all Thy creatures, we desire to have a higher conception of the world of nature and humanity. These heavens bending over us at night with a thousand twinkling lights are so quietly friendly that we would not miss the message they breathe. We thank Thee for varicolored clouds of sunset wonder, for mountain majesties, for tasseling corn fields, for mirroring waters, for daisy-dotted meadows – surely they are expressions of the Divine. "Day unto day uttereth speech, and night unto night showeth knowledge." And if Thou dost give heavenly tongues to grasses of the fields, surely men, whom Thou hast made, are full of Thy speech. "Spirit with spirit can meet." Through the nobler gates of some of Thy sons and daughters Thou art pouring fuller tides of Thy intelligence and power and love than through others – but teach us that the smallest child is a Divine word and the most despised man is a whole message of Thine. May we honor Thy word in others and fulfill it in ourselves. For Jesus' sake. Amen.

VACATION DAYS AND WAYS

He hath made everything beautiful in its time
—Ecclesiastes 3:11

Our Father God, we bless Thee today that Thou art not only our Father, but that Thou art our Creator, and "the Creator of the ends of the earth." We thank Thee for "the beauty of the earth and the glory of the skies." We bless Thee for eyes to see the Unseen in the seen, and find Thee everywhere. Our Lord, make these vacation days times when our tired minds and bodies shall be rested, and when our depleted spiritual sense shall be renewed. May the heavens declare to us the glory of God and the firmament show us His handiwork. May the Christ, who sailed and walked in Galilee remind us that "the sea is his," and that He made the dry ground. May every mountain-spot Thy children see remind them of His prayer and His preaching upon the mountainside, and through all our journeying days and ways, may God Himself keep "our going out and our coming in, from this time forth and even forevermore." For the sake of Christ. Amen.

†

THANKSGIVING

And Jesus answering said, Were not the ten cleansed? but where are the nine? Were there none found that returned to give glory to God, save this stranger? –Luke 17:17, 18

Lord of the harvest, help us as individual souls, as families, communities, and a nation to keep faith with Thee at this Thanksgiving season. What a constant and bountiful Giver Thou art! May we never repeat the meanness of the lepers who heedlessly failed to give thanks to the Master who healed them. May we have the grace both to think and to speak our gratitude for a thousand mercies more than we have deserved. May Thanksgiving Day never be limited to a round of festivities and amusements, but may our first and our last thought be one of overflowing thanks, for the harvest blessings, for the national good, and for all the tender things of human experience. Even if this particular year has been full of distresses and burdens, yet, Lord, if by Thy help we have been able to we will praise Thee, as the "help of our countenance and our God." Amen.

THANKSGIVING DAY

Rejoice in the Lord, ye righteous; and give thanks at the remembrance of his holiness
—Psalm 97:12.

O bountiful Father, what shall we render unto Thee for all Thy benefits? "Thou openest thine hand and satisfiest the desire of every living thing." "Thou upholdest all that fall." "Thou crownest the year with thy goodness." Every year is a marvel and a delight as its scroll unfolds from the Hand of beauty and love: the bloom of Spring, the glow of Summer, the gorgeous show of Autumn, the rich harvests gathered in cellar, barn, and bin. Joyous praises fill our hearts as we think of a year's prosperity and peace, of health and home and love, of brave deeds planned and brave deeds done, and faith and hope and love which have not deceived us. O God, as one of our seers has said, "we would put ourselves at zero and then reckon every degree ascending from that point as an occasion for thanks." "Bless the Lord, O my soul, who crowneth thee with loving kindness and tender mercies." Amen.

OUR THANKSGIVING INHERITANCE

Ye shall divide the land for inheritance . . . and ye shall inherit it, one as well as another
—Ezekiel 47:13, 14

O God, we are grateful for that progressive and constructive spirit permeating our country which has felled forests, built cities, and increased resources until the land has been filled with the good things of an advanced civilization. And yet, O Lord, what have we that we did not receive? Thou didst prepare these goodly plains and mountains. Thou didst make the soil rich and didst fill the mountains with gold and silver, copper and iron. Yea, and our fathers paid a price for "the decencies, securities, and opportunities" which we at present enjoy. May we be conscious that there are certain political, social, and cultural blessings that we did not win for ourselves but which are now our most fixed and precious traditions. May we be decently appreciative of what the past has wrought for us, and, as we are proud of our inheritance, give us a fitting ambition to be worthy of it. Lord, give us more than this; help us also to end some great injustice or to install some great benefit so that later generations shall rise up and call us blessed, as we bless the fathers. In Christ's Name. Amen.

HARVEST

Praise Jehovah, O Jerusalem;
Praise thy God, O Zion.
He maketh peace in thy borders;
He filleth thee with the finest of the wheat
—Psalm 147:12, 14

O Heavenly Father, Thy children bring to Thee the joy of harvest. It is Thou who dost give not only the fruitful soil, but also the golden sunlight and the refreshing rains. Thou dost inspire the secret processes of growth. The earth is Thy marvelous laboratory where Thou dost produce all that man needs for food and drink, for clothing and shelter. And now, as the earth has once more brought forth its increase and as all fear of dearth or scarcity has again been removed, we bow humbly before Thee to bless Thee for Thy divine goodness. As the song of the reaper has been heard in the land, so may there now be the voice of melody and heartfelt praise in a thousand hearts. Grant that, as we receive Thy bountiful gifts, we may know how to employ the same for Thy honor. In the Name of the Great Benefactor. Amen.

GRATITUDE FOR HARVEST

And he shall be like a tree planted by the
streams of water,
That bringeth forth its fruit in its season,
Whose leaf also doth not wither;
And whatsoever he doeth shall prosper
—Psalm 1:3

Gracious Lord, the bountiful Giver of all good, we acknowledge with thankfulness that goodness and mercy have followed us all the days of our life. We thank Thee for the products of the field and the increase of the flocks. The silver and the gold are Thine, and the cattle on a thousand hills. Many gifts from summer and autumn are in our hand. Accumulated bounties of other years make our lives rich with plenty. Whatever we get or fail to get from the work of our hands and from the disposals of Thy providence, may the instinctive response of our hearts to the orderings of our lot be that Thou art God and Thou art good. May we believe in Thy unchangeable love and joyfully claim the grace of responding filial love as one of our chief duties. May we learn a fuller life with Thee, and attain a closer walk with God. Through Him who first loved us. Amen.

THE BRIDLED TONGUE

There is that speaketh rashly like the piercings
of a sword;
But the tongue of the wise is health
—Proverbs 12:18

Teach us, O Lord, that life and death are in words as well as deeds, that "a grievous word stirreth up strife" while gracious words are like "apples of gold in vessels of silver." Keep us ever closely observing Him upon whose lips ever dwelt "the law of kindness." We confess the cold and deadly words that we have often addressed to others. We confess also the cynical and carping words about others. We are sorry and ashamed today for every idle word we have uttered and we implore Thy forgiveness. Fill our hearts with a new feeling for our fellows, and our mouths with the music of gentle speech. May we possess within us the merry heart which "doeth good like a medicine" and may our "lips o'erflow with grace." In the Name of Jesus. Amen.

THE TONGUE

Death and life are in the power of the tongue
—Proverbs 18:21

Why, O Lord, should we add thoughtlessly to the sorrows of life when there are already more than many can bear? We hurt one another. Others hurt us. Wounds are inflicted everywhere, as if we did not realize that although a wound may heal, the scar remains. As we have suffered perhaps through decades from hurts inflicted upon us as little children, from slights in youth, from treacheries in later years, lend caution to our tongues and compassion to our hearts that we may not inflict irremediable injury upon our fellows. Help us rather to smooth their path, rough enough already; establish their courage, beset enough by oppositions as it is; and sweeten their cup, bitter enough at best. May we no longer devour one another after the fashion of the beasts but, as we handle human nature, give us the velvety touch of the Master, who has been called "the most perfect gentleman that ever breathed." In His Name. Amen.

TRUTH-TELLING

Speak ye every man the truth with his neighbor . . . . love no false oath; for all these are things that I hate, saith Jehovah

—Zechariah 8:16, 17

We thank Thee, Lord Jesus, that men have addressed Thee as the "Crystal Christ," because in Thee they found no blemish of untruth. But we lament that outside of Christendom so much of the world still declines to call a lie wrong and excuses it as a venial sin. If a higher standard prevails in Europe and America, we know who has established it. We thank Thee that, whereas in trade lying was once thought indispensable, it has given place to so much dealing that is straightforward. We thank Thee for the whole institution of credit, based, as it is, upon truthfulness. We thank Thee that, whereas bargaining among backward peoples is expressed in artful deceit, where Thy influence is felt we may buy with confidence from an advertisement. Help us to guard with jealousy this pearl of great price. May we realize that by minor deviations from the truth we may lose it. Help us to loathe social lies, political lies, and acted lies. So may we rise from the truth in lesser things to the great fact of Him, who is the Way, the Truth and the Life. Amen.

THE BLESSED TREES

Praise Jehovah from the earth, . . .
Mountains, and all hills;
Fruitful trees, and all cedars; . . .
Let them praise the name of Jehovah

—Psalm 148:7, 9, 13

It gives us pause, O Lord, to realize that there were satisfaction and pleasure in the heart of Thee the Eternal when Thou lookedst upon the primeval forests and orchards and divine joy at the sight of the green world Thou hadst made. Thou foundest the woods congenial in the cool of the day. As we observe in the trees evidences of the mind of the Maker, devices within them that pull and lift, exerting magic pressures, assuming intricate and fascinating colors and shapes, making astonishing chemical combinations, anticipating trouble, repairing damage, and storing for the future, may all this mystic sensitivity and power give us an enhanced wonder at the glory and greatness of the all-wise Creator. Glory be to Thee, O God! We can trust Thy provision for us in this world and that which is to come. Hallelujah! Amen.

THE TREES

And out of the ground made Jehovah God to grow every tree that is pleasant to the sight, and good for food; the tree of life also in the midst of the garden, and the tree of the knowledge of good and evil –Genesis 2:9

O Thou great Builder of our world-home with all its glories and delights, we bless Thee that Thou didst, in creation's dawn, plant a garden in Eden and fill it with trees that were pleasant to behold and useful for man. We thank Thee for the groves, the first temples. May we never lose our reverence for the work of Thy hands but rather behold Thee and Thy thought in all that breathes, or moves, or grows. If we have too freely spent the rich and magnificent gift that Nature bestowed on us by stripping our forests, permitting devastating fires, and destroying young growth, forgive us for wasting Thy dowry and remind us of the thrift of Him who, after the feeding of the five thousand, gave instructions, saying, "Gather up the fragments that remain." Amen.

UNITY

Behold, how good and how pleasant it is
For brethren to dwell together in unity!
—Psalm 133:1

We thank Thee, O God, for the progress the race has made from the days of savage individualism, when every man's hand was raised against every other's, to the present age of organized society. We thank Thee for all the men and women of world outlook who are disregarding racial, national, religious, and political boundaries and putting emphasis upon the fundamental agreements of modern society. May we never shrink from decent controversy, knowing that final truth can be attained only in this way. Yet give us a feeling of respect for our brother's sincerity and of fellowship with him in all wherein he and we agree. Rebuke the indolent and superficial attitude that all convictions, theories, and faiths are equally good, but rebuke also the intolerant assumption that any party, cult, or race is excluded from some place in the Providential plan for the development of humanity. In the Name of Jesus Christ, the World Comrade. Amen.

UNITY

He made of one every nation of men to dwell on all the face of the earth —Acts 17:26

Forgive us, O Lord, that after all these centuries of the Christian era, and with all the broadening influences of our modern life, we are still inclined to keep our sympathies within limited horizons of class, creed, and nation. Some of us are narrow and bigoted. Some are bitter and hard. Some are haughty and Pharisaical. Some are vindictive. But we "have not so learned Christ." We thank Thee for His brotherly ways, thoughts, and deeds. We thank Thee for His constant efforts to push out men's horizons and for the breadth of a mind which not only went beyond the narrow villagers of His day, but which also challenges in this more advanced age the leaders of the human race. Give us a deepening appreciation of the outreach of Jesus' ideas and a constant thankfulness for their perennial fitness for whatever new situations the new centuries bring. May we recall how He said: "If ye know those things, happy are ye if ye do them." In His Name. Amen.

UNITY

Till we all attain unto the unity of the faith

—Ephesians 4:13

Hear the confession of Thy Church, O Lord, that we are divided into so many sects instead of being one as the Saviour prayed. We are acting under the false stimulus of exclusive group ambition instead of that perfect love toward others and Thee which Jesus commanded. Prejudice, hatred, and fear have displaced the primitive apostolic elements of understanding, sympathy, and cooperation. Give us a deep and reverent anxiety that prejudice shall melt away, that tradition shall be shorn of its power, and that moral nearsightedness shall be displaced by a universal vision of the common inner objectives of unrelated movements in the Christian world. Bestow upon us that humility which conditions all reception of truth and all possibility of growth. As the survival values of the Church are being so searchingly examined, give us the judgment of the Spirit that we may continue to approve only that which is excellent. Hasten the day, we beseech Thee, of universal Christian harmony and, if it be Thy will, may we finally attain in Thy good pleasure to organic Christian unity. In Christ's Name. Amen.

VETERANS' DAY

And it shall come to pass in the latter days, that the mountain of Jehovah's house shall be established on the top of the mountains, . . . and all nations shall flow unto it . . . And He will judge between the nations, and will decide concerning many peoples

—Isaiah 2:2, 4

O Lord of all peoples, multiply the number of those in every nation who definitely strive to create a public opinion averse to war. Confound the counsels of backward-looking men who have no hope or vision concerning a better day. Bless every educational endeavor to spread the facts concerning the origin, conduct, and consequences of the wars of the past. May each of us strive to be at peace with his neighbor. Help us to "seek peace and pursue it." May the individual lovers of peace be mobilized into such a mighty host of brothers that no suspicion or greed or intrigue or pride of those who guide national destinies can successfully stand against it. So may civilization finally reach the Holy City of God. In the Name of the Prince of Peace. Amen.

VETERANS' DAY

Then said Hezekiah unto Isaiah, Good is the word of Jehovah which thou hast spoken. He said moreover, Is it not so, if peace and truth shall be in my days —II Kings 20:19

O God, give us faith to feel that the primal push behind all social evolution is the Divine hand moving in love. We thank Thee for unnumbered millions the world over who are today cherishing the vision of a world without war. We thank Thee for so much intelligence, leadership, and courage in the high places of every land consecrated to this end. If apologists for war tell us that nature is unchangeable and that war alone can keep hardihood and heroism alive, may we contend for peace, remembering the long way we have come from the epochs of "tooth and claw" and the opportunity we have to change battles with our fellow men into battles for them. May we conserve any values of war by mobilizing our energies against the difficulties and injustices of life and exchange the glamor of war for the romance of social betterment. Help us to think peace, talk peace, and live peaceably with our neighbors. Bless every prophet and statesman, every group and government the world over, that appreciates the folly, waste, and crime of war and seeks to substitute for the final suicide of civilization the final Truce of God. In Jesus' Name. Amen.

†

THE PATRIOTISM OF WASHINGTON

Ask now of the days that are past, which were before thee. . . . God [hath] assayed to go and take him a nation from the midst of another nation, . . . by war, and by a mighty hand
—Deuteronomy 4:32, 34

How can we find words, O Lord, to thank Thee for him who was a commander of armies, the father of a people and the first of our Presidents? Thou didst bless him with an iron frame bound by nerves of steel and didst set within him a great heart; but he did not consider the gifts of intelligence and physique, of birth and wealth, evidences of a divine favoritism but rather indications of a great service to be rendered his fellow men. How ambitious for his country, how regardless for himself! In this our day when men are disagreed as to what patriotism is and what patriotism requires, help us find an answer in the character and career of Washington. May we love the commonweal as did he. Give us a civic virtue which, like his, seizes principle and applies it at any cost, which suffers sacrifice without conscious martydom, which bears calumny without reply, which is successful without ambition, which is resisted without resentment, and which is never cast down by adversity nor lifted up to arrogance in prosperity. In the Name of Washington's God. Amen.

THE PERSEVERANCE OF WASHINGTON

Stir up the gift of God, which is in thee. . . . For God gave us not a spirit of fearfulness; but of power and love and discipline

–II Timothy 1:6, 7

We bless Thee, O God, the Ruler of nations, that "our fathers brought forth on this continent a new nation, conceived in liberty and dedicated to the proposition that all men are created equal"; and we are especially grateful for the sublime devotion displayed by the Father of his country. We commemorate his faith, his resolution, and his iron will when the frail structure of the new republic seemed about to collapse. We thank Thee that he never gave up though the national credit and the army's morale were failing him. Bestow upon our leaders of today some of this same lofty spirit. Let none despair because of difficulties. Show us that when we project our lives out along the lines of God's will, we have the promise, "If God be for us, who can be against us?" So gird us about that we shall push forward, knowing that what ought to be done can be done. In the Name of the Author and Finisher of our faith. Amen.

WINTER WANES

For, lo, the winter is past;
The rain is over and gone

—Song of Solomon 2:11

Our hearts are awed within us, and we offer to Thee, the Mightiest, our humble praise as we think of the great miracle that goes on in silence around us. Untold centuries have come and gone, yet seed-time and harvest, winter and summer have never failed. "For Art may err, but Nature cannot miss." O God, when Thou dost send the hard, dull bitterness of cold with rushing blasts from the North, or dismal rains coming down in slanting lines, when Thou dost withdraw the genial sun and shorten our days, when Thou dost cause dumb hearts to hide behind the pulseless trees, then indeed do we observe the sterner aspects of Thy law. Yet, O God, we know that beneath the snow Nature's breath is warm as ever. Dainty violets sleep safely through the churlish winter. The birds are only truants. They will return. We bless Thee that even now there is a new and serenely tender light in the sky and Spring bends archly to catch our glance. The night is melting with the morn and we will rejoice in God our Saviour! Amen.

†

WINTER'S BLESSING

Out of the chamber of the south cometh the storm,
And cold out of the north —Job 37:9

When the landscape is bleak and the biting cold chills every limb and we think of the suffering of exposed workers and of the poor, it is hard for us to be thankful for Winter. Yet, though the tempest of sleet and snow rages and we are caught in the grip of the blizzard, teach us that Winter has its place in Thy plan. Thou doest all things well. We marvel at the inexhaustible shapes of beauty formed by Thy brush and we should be poorer in our knowledge of Thee without the immaculate whiteness of the snow. We thank Thee for Winter's sports; the tingling blood of the skater, the joy of coasting children. We thank Thee for deep snows in the fields assuring fertility and bread for human life. We thank Thee for the secret ministries of the frost and the cold. Thy ways are higher than our ways. Let us meet every spiritual winter with the same faith, and bring us all at last to the eternal Spring. In the Name of Thy Son, our Lord. Amen.

THE BREAK-UP OF WINTER

As the rain cometh down and the snow from heaven, and . . . watereth the earth, and maketh it bring forth and bud —Isaiah 55:10, 11

We thank Thee, our gracious Father, that light springeth up in the darkness; that the graciousness of the flower is enfolded within the tight grip of the bud; that all hard seasons are times of secret growth; that the shadowed and frozen months of Winter nourish the violets and ferns, the fruits of the orchard and field, and all the wealth of summer glory. "Thou hast made summer and winter." Now, O Lord, as we are emerging from the cold, cutting disciplines of Winter, may we have hearts full of gratitude for the days behind with their providential meanings and the days ahead for all they will bring of sunshine and comfort. May the process of divine culture be forwarded by all our experience. May our distresses drive us to Thy sheltering love. May our blessings be seasons of gratitude and devotion. May we gather strength and nutriment for our spirits "in season and out." In Jesus' Name. Amen.

Part II

Miscellaneous Religious Themes

THE ALTRUISTIC LIFE

Not looking each of you to his own things, but each of you also to the things of others
—Philippians 2:4

We desire to confess to Thee, O Lord God, that many of us are so absorbed in our private affairs that we ignore the calls to serve the common good. We leave it to others to solve the problem of wretched housing, of futile police departments, of deficient schools, or corrupt politics, and many other public interests. May we be neither so selfish nor so mistaken as to think that getting and spending are the whole of life. Remind us of the evidence of Christian behavior set up by the Master in His parable concerning sick people, prisoners, and the poor. Point out to each one of us his opportunity not only to help secure justice, honesty, and efficiency in civic affairs, but also to visit the sick, clothe the naked, feed the hungry, and perform other deeds of humanity for those who cross our path, or whom we can help by some other means. So may we be like Him who "went about doing good." In His Name. Amen.

AS ONE THAT SERVETH

The Son of man came not to be ministered unto, but to minister, and to give his life a ransom for many —Matthew 20:28

When we sing, "Joy to the World, the Lord is come!" help us among our various causes for rejoicing to recall that Jesus came to exhibit a new type of manhood, one whose purpose was to give rather than to get. As we remember how, before He came, the masterful man who could conquer and reign was the man who received homage, we glory in the humble circumstances of Jesus' birth, the spirit of His life, and the vicarious suffering of His death. We bless Thee that all the rare flowerings of human devotion and unselfishness preceding His coming were but the earnest of the ever-blooming and gorgeous Rose of Sharon, of which the spirit of sacrificial service is leaf and stem and root. May His clear vision of the oneness of humanity steadily become the ideal of all men. May all individual, corporate, or national selfishness find more and more that it is existing in defiance of fundamental morality. May the leaven of Jesus' spirit finally imbue the life of humanity with the quality of its own. So may Thy will be done on earth as it is in heaven. Amen.

ASSURANCE OF IMMORTALITY

For it was the good pleasure of the Father . . . through [*Christ*] *to reconcile all things unto himself, having made peace through the blood of his cross; through him, I say, whether things upon the earth, or things in the heavens*

—Colossians 1:19, 20

O Sovereign Wisdom, who art also our heavenly Father, what a marvelous thing it is that Thou hast stamped upon each human soul Thine own image, and hast endowed it with a ray of perfect wisdom. Thou hast set an inextinguishable light in mortal bodies and placed the instinct of permanent existence in our poor human hearts. We cannot believe that this nobler part of us dies when the body decays. We are grateful to note that often the most suffering body is the home of the most advancing soul. We remember how the Psalmist exclaimed, "My flesh and my heart faileth; but God is the strength of my heart and my portion for ever." As Thou dost destroy no least atom of the universe, as "not a sparrow falleth on the ground without our Father," we will rise above all fears, all tears, all doubt, and even all sin, and face the future mystery unafraid, because Thou hast made man to be the image of Thine own eternity. In the Name of the great Lord of life. Amen.

AUSPICIOUS HOPE

But now abideth . . . hope –I Corinthians 13:13

We thank Thee, heavenly Father, that in the Kingdom of Christ no one ever loses his all. No human soul is ever bankrupt and beyond redemption. The stories of Jesus' life show us that however a man may be driven to bay by the assaults of his own evil nature or the persecutions of others, yet some undefeatable principle is always left, and he can yet be "more than conqueror." We thank Thee that, whatever the lapses of any lives, whatever the decay of faith, whatever the moral defeats, none of us is ever out of reach of the "everlasting arms." May the thief on the cross and the prodigal in the far country ever remind us that something always remains in us which can be touched into life. Instead of being spiritual paupers, we can possess the unsearchable riches of Christ. Save erring sons or daughters today through the sinner's Friend, Jesus Christ, the "Lamb of God who taketh away the sin of the world." Amen.

BALANCED OPTIMISM

Fear not, little flock; for it is your Father's good pleasure to give you the kingdom –Luke 12:32

Help us, O Lord, to see clearly the facts regarding ourselves and others. We thank Thee that Jesus was not superficially hopeful for humanity because He did not understand the real evils inherent in it or the tragic situation of this particular time, but that with His eyes open to all the dark realities of life about Him, He nevertheless cried, "Ye believe in God; believe also in me!" and He gave assurance to His hearers. May we have confidence in the penetration of One who could tell the story of the Prodigal Son. Give us more of the insight of Jesus. May we never be so alarmed by any view of things as they are, though we see how bad the situation really is. May we never give place to the cynic. We thank Thee for the testimony of revelation and history that "with God all things are possible." May Thy Holy Spirit fill us with "all joy in believing." In Jesus' Name. Amen.

BEING A FRIEND

I have called you friends –John 15:15

O Lord, give us high ideals of friendship, and help us to enjoy as the best gift of life the love and service of others. Deliver us from friendships that are shallow, passing, and worthless. Reveal to us genuine human worth in our midst. As we admire others, give us the impulse to benefit them rather than to seek benefit from them. Help us to abhor friendships which simply exist to trade favors. May we keep no books and send in no accounts, but delight to minister to others with unwearying affection. And may we have such depth of love for others that we shall be concerned for their highest good. Even at the risk of losing our friends, may we be brave to advise, to rebuke, to warn. May we never be content to do the small and easy parts of friendship without being willing to perform its duties. Endow us with such sincerity that, if we must give pain, it will be said of us, "Faithful are the wounds of a friend." In the Name of Jesus, our Divine Friend. Amen.

THE BEST

Now we see in a mirror, darkly
—I Corinthians 13:12

Remind us, O Lord, that if Jesus taught us to "seek first the kingdom of God" and Paul urged us to "approve things that are excellent," we should examine and test all values in life to see if they are true or false. May we examine our schooling to learn whether it is producing that wisdom which is "the principal thing." If riches increase, may we not set our heart upon them. Deliver us from loving the praise of men more than the praise of God. Reveal especially to our youth the superiority of a good conscience to a passing thrill of pleasure. May we excel in wise choices by closely following in the steps of our Master. Amen.

BROTHERHOOD OF THE RACE

And I, if I be lifted up from the earth, will draw all men unto myself —John 12:32

O Thou, who dost make Thy "sun to rise on the evil and the good, and sendeth rain on the just and the unjust," we thank Thee for the glorious reflection of the Father's interest in humanity which we find in the life and teachings of Christ. We thank Thee for His fondness for the title, Son of man. We thank Thee not only for His treatment of blind paupers, harlots, and sinners of His own people, but for His attitude toward idol-worshipping foreigners and even red-handed Romans doing Him to His death. Oh, wonderful love of Christ, ignoring the accidents of race, culture, and moral development! May the Christian world learn from Thee that "there cannot be Greek and Jew, barbarian, Scythian, bondman, freeman: but Christ is all and in all." May we move forward with chastened tenderness to Christlike standards and see in every man a child of the Father. In Jesus' Name. Amen.

BURDENS

Out of the depths have I cried unto thee, O Jehovah.
Lord, hear my voice:
Let thine ears be attentive
To the voice of my supplications

—Psalm 130:1, 2

O God, who art mindful of Thy children everywhere, remember in Thy loving-kindness those of us upon whom the heavy burdens of sickness, separation, poverty, or grief have fallen. "The sorrows of death have compassed us and the pains of hell have taken hold of us." We have found trouble and sorrow. All Thy waves and thy billows have gone over us. Yet, O Lord, we would look to Thee as our sure Deliverer, a Rock of Defense to save us. Thou canst deliver our souls from death, our eyes from tears, and our feet from falling. Save now, we beseech Thee, O Lord, and our mouths shall show forth Thy praise. So may we witness a good confession of fidelity and faith before many witnesses who shall know that there is a God in Israel. In Jesus' Name. Amen.

THE CHALLENGE OF MYSTERY

Then shall we know, if we follow on to know the Lord: his going forth is prepared as the morning –Hosea 6:3.

O Lord God, if this is a strange and singular world to us, full of mysteries, sorrows, and enigmas we cannot explain, if we are tantalized by happenings whose meanings are hidden and by anomalies in nature, if there are veils we cannot tear aside and dreams we cannot interpret – enable us humbly to recognize that Thy ways are higher than our ways and Thy thoughts than our thoughts. Yet we would not rest satisfied. Teach us the way of daily inquiry. Enable us always to keep on "the line of discovery." May knowledge grow from more to more. Thou dost make secrets of things to show them to us more plainly after a while. May patience, search, and trust have their perfect work until the wisdom and glory of hidden things are fully revealed. In Jesus' Name. Amen.

CHEAP RELIGION

And [David] said, . . . neither will I offer burnt-offerings unto Jehovah my God which cost me nothing –II Samuel 24:24

We are ashamed of ourselves, our Father, when we contrast Thy devotion to us with our devotion to Thee Thou didst not spare Thine only Son but didst freely give

Him up for us all. We grudge Thee a quarter of a day or a trifling gift of money. Thou dost stand in the night patiently knocking at our hearts; but we are too busy with our own matters to hear. Thou dost forgive us seventy times seven, but we turn upon Thee in bad humor with the first experience of loss, disappointment, or sorrow. We read, "The ox knoweth his owner, and the ass his master's crib; but Israel doth not know, my people doth not consider." Alas, O Lord, that our instincts of fellowship and of gratitude should sometimes be excelled even by the faithful animals of the household or farm. With genuine contrition may we renew our vows of faith and love, nor longer offer Thee the leftovers of time and talent, of means and fellowship, but in exchange of Thine all, give Thee our all. In Jesus' Name. Amen.

CHEERFULNESS

A merry heart doeth good like a medicine: but a broken spirit drieth the bones

—Proverbs 17:22.

We are glad, our heavenly Father, that Jesus Christ is the true Light, "lightening every man that cometh into the world." We praise Thee that in Him is no darkness at all, no shadows of resentment, envy, complaint, or fear. We rejoice to feel that He was bouyant, yea, radiant. Give us Jesus' spirit. Fill us with sunshine like the flowers. May our smiles cast a golden hue about us. To this end let us obey Thee as Jesus did. Let us walk with Thee in the fever as well as "the cool of the day." Then, out of a well-ordered soul, music shall flow; out of a holy purpose, brightness shall glow; and out of central depths of divine fellowship shall spring a well of water to refresh the thirsty souls around us. So make us like our adorable Lord! Amen.

CHRISTIAN COMMON SENSE

Now speakest thou plainly. . . . Now know we that thou knowest all things –John 16:29, 30

Heavenly Father, we praise Thee that, while so many of our minds are unbalanced to a greater or less degree, yet no critic has ever found a mole or a flaw in the mind of Christ. We thank Thee for His insistence that His followers should use their reason. Help us to do so. May we not argue about Christianity when we have never read the life of its Founder. May we not neglect acquaintance with the one source of authentic information as to what the Christian religion actually is. As we read the Gospels, "Open thou our eyes to behold wondrous things out of thy law," and may we discover in the common sense of Jesus' teachings how full and rich and wonderful He meant life to be. For His sake. Amen.

THE CHURCH UNIVERSAL

Christ . . . loved the church, and gave himself up for it –Ephesians 5:25

Lord Jesus, teach us that, although the Church is composed of fallible men and women, and is often erring, feeble, and divided, yet in the purpose of God it is the body and bride of His only Son. Help us to understand that the Church is the medium of Thy revelation, the organ through which truth for the seeking soul, guidance for a stumbling civilization, and comfort for weary hearts everywhere are mediated by Almighty God. May the Church ever prove a noble nursery for youth; a perennial fountain of healing waters; oracles of a wisdom pure and peaceable, coming down from above; a pillar and ground of the truth. Here may we, like the Prodigal Son, find ourselves. May we escape the pull of today's thinking which would draw us down into the whole of nature or the whole of society. May we hold fast, standing before God unafraid because of our Divine Sponsor, Jesus Christ. Help us to give to the Church not our names, or our money, or our physical presence, but our souls and our all. In the Name of Him who loved the Church and gave Himself for it. Amen.

COMBATIVE COURAGE

Suffer hardship . . . , as a good soldier of Jesus Christ –II Timothy 2:3

We thank Thee for the courageous personality of Jesus Christ and for all the men of oak and iron and all the women of sustained heroism whom He has inspired. We thank Thee that the resistance of humanity has not been confined to the battlefield. We thank Thee for Stevensons, who have fought a game fight with malignant disease, for Lincolns, who have resisted letters blistered with tears in the performance of duty, for Savonerolas, who have given their lives pleading for righteousness and for hosts of lesser men and women, who, in blindness, have made their living, in sickness have smiled, in poverty have endured, in disappointment have been steadfast, and in mediocrity have done their best. Help us, O Lord, to do likewise. Though we lose our children, though wasting disease overtakes us, though fortune collapses, give us that combative courage that carries on against all obstacles. May we be "faint, yet pursuing" like the undiscourageable apostle of old. In the Name of Him who "set his face stedfastly to go up to Jerusalem." Amen.

COMRADE CROSSES

To you it hath been granted in the behalf of Christ, not only to believe on him, but also to suffer in his behalf –Philippians 1:29

Oh, the crosses, Thou Crucified One, that have stood beside Thine in all the centuries since Thou wast so cruelly impaled on Golgotha! Surely, O Lord Jesus, Thou hast not died in vain! In all lands and in every corner of the earth there have been noble souls who have not been content to be healthy and wealthy and privileged and happy, who have not counted their lives dear unto themselves, but who have learned the truth of the Saviour's paradox and have given in order to get, have lost in order to gain, and have died in order to live. May the fine generation of youth coming upon our scene today not journey toward Sodom, but join the procession up the slopes of Calvary and plant their crosses beside His who knew the only way by which the race could be saved. In the Name of Christ. Amen.

CONVERSION

That which is born of the flesh is flesh; and that which is born of the Spirit is spirit. . . . Ye must be born anew. –John 3:6, 7

We bless Thee, O God, that Jesus Christ can transform human lives. We thank Thee that evil desire can disappear, that hatred can change to love, and that a new outlook upon God and man and destiny can displace the narrow horizon of the past. We thank Thee that divine spiritual power can seize the soul and change the heart of stone to a heart of flesh. May this great renewal, in which, through the action of God's Spirit, honor, purity, and truth, as they appeared in Christ's life, become the chief good, be experienced by thousands of men and women. Deliver us from superficial explanations of the fact of conversion and strengthen the belief that the life of God can flow in like a tide upon the shores of humanity. May the power of Jesus Christ to conquer weakness, overcome prejudice, and bring a better life in men's souls be evidenced more and more by those who claim to be His followers; and may they carry their message of deliverance and hope to others. In Jesus' Name. Amen.

CORPORATE INTERCESSION

Neither shall there be mourning, nor crying, nor pain, any more —Revelation 21:4

Hear our prayers, O Lord, not for ourselves, needy though we be, but for the whole great family of which we are a part. Help the sick. Give them patience. Grant recovery if Thou deemest wise. Make Thou their bed in their sickness and comfort them as a mother comforts her child. Bless absent loved ones and friends. Keep them from danger and harm. May the Angel of Thy presence be with them wherever they are. Bless all households passing through deep waters. May their afflictions cause them more than ever to love one another with a pure heart fervently, and may their tears be as lenses through which they may more clearly glimpse Thy face. Follow with Thy Spirit's solicitations every prodigal son or daughter. Bless Thy holy Church Universal that Thy saving health may be known among all nations. Bless our President and every other officer, lawmaker, or judge, that our land may abide in righteousness, peace, and prosperity. In Christ's Name. Amen.

DEADENING ROUTINE

Whatsoever ye do, work heartily, . . . knowing that . . . ye serve the Lord Christ

—Colossians 3:23, 24

Thou knowest, O Lord, that, as we labor each day for our daily bread, working in the same store or office, or at the same trade, or repeating the same household tasks, we feel the deadening influence of routine. Our finest faculties sicken and weaken under the process which involves a monotonous task. Show us how to escape the danger of dulled hopes, blunted sensibilities, and commonplace thinking. In our better moments we know that all things are possible with Thee, and that Jesus is able to make all grace abound unto us. May every human task be glorified and every human contact be freshened by the love and peace and vision which He can bestow. In His Name. Amen.

DIVINE CONCEALMENT

It is the glory of God to conceal a thing

—Proverbs 25:2

We reverently acknowledge, O Lord God, that Thy ways are higher than our ways, and Thy thoughts than our thoughts. Thou hast enveloped Thyself in a cloud. Thou hast hidden precious secrets of nature for us to find. Thou hast fringed all reality with mystery. We know only in part. But we gladly acquiesce in this Thy divine plane of concealing the values of time and eternity. As we therefore proceed further in this adventure of life, remind us that the great is concealed in the small, that truth is hidden in experience, that time is enveloped in eternity, and that "eye hath not seen, nor ear heard, neither have entered into the heart of man, the things which God hath prepared for them that love him." In Jesus' Name. Amen.

ENDURANCE

Be ye stedfast, unmovable, always abounding in the work of the Lord, forasmuch as ye know that your labor is not vain in the Lord
—I Corinthians 15:58

O Lord our Maker, when we pause in our busy lives, we realize it is a strange scheme of circumstances in which we have been set. Clouds of mystery hide our origin and a veil is over our future. At times, the desert plod makes life seem but a weary waste. Now we are sad, and now the song of a bird or a child brings music to our hearts. Preserve us from the perils of our lot. Keep wonder and reverence alive. Help us not to become used to sin or deceived by glamour, but rather to know that crystal streams, healing trees, and an eternal City of the Beautiful is all about us, were our eyes washed with the Spirit to see. May we bear up a little longer. Keep us steadfast despite the pettiness of men, the fret of care, the cruel toil, and the misunderstandings and strife. Help us still to "do justly, to love kindness, and to walk humbly with our God." Amen.

FORBEARANCE

Why dost thou judge thy brother? . . . or why dost thou set at naught thy brother

—Romans 14:10

O Thou great Father of the human family, heal that blindness of ours which fails to see how different Thou hast made everything and everybody in this world. We thank Thee that we are not minted, but each one is handmade of Thee, and enjoys a special fitting to a particular purpose or place. Help us not to fret ourselves so much because we cannot make others conform to our likeness. May we not have so much pride in our own ways of thought or behavior, in our own creed or party or standards, that we ignore Thy creative hand in the diversities which mark other lives. Make us less sure of ourselves till we have cast the beam out of our own eye and are more ready to believe that perhaps there is only a mote in our brother's eye. Keep us from being so hard on one another. In the Name of the compassionate Christ. Amen.

FOREIGN MISSIONS

Only be strong and very courageous, . . . that thou mayest have good success whithersoever thou goest. . . . Have not I commanded thee? Be strong and of good courage; be not affrighted, neither be thou dismayed: for Jehovah thy God is with thee withersoever thou goest

—Joshua 1:7, 8, 9

Our father's God and our God, we thank Thee for the heroic Christian generations of past ages who, through faith and courage wrought righteousness, subdued kingdoms of evil, and even at the loss of their own blood established our holy religion in the earth. We bless Thee for men and women of today who are zealous for the faith; who have compassion upon distant multitudes, without hope and without God; and who are willing to risk fevers or mobs in order that they may "rescue the perishing." God, bless these noble men and women of our time and inspire others just as courageous to arise from among our youth and, like good volunteers for Christ, to exclaim, "Here am I. Send me!" In the Name of Him who came to seek and save the lost. Amen.

FORGIVING MEN

If ye forgive men their trespasses, your heavenly Father will also forgive you —Matthew 6:14

Help us, O Lord, not to be quite so sure about our own forgiveness by Thee if we have not been forgiving to others. May we search and know our own hearts and "see if there be any evil way" in us. In the difficult matter of maintaining a Christian spirit when we are suffering from being wronged, keep us ever in living touch with Him "who though he was reviled, reviled not again, though he suffered, threatened not." If we must endure financial loss, mortified pride, or wounded sensibilities at the hands of an enemy, deliver us, we pray Thee, from cherishing any temper of revenge or even from harboring resentment. Yea, even give us that chivalrous magnanimity that is more than pardon, that spirit that opens the door for our brother's return, that sense of hungering for fellowship that includes even those who have "despitefully used us and persecuted us." So shall Jesus Christ through us win the victory! In His Name. Amen.

FORTITUDE

Christ also suffered for you, leaving you an example, . . . who when he was reviled, reviled not again; when he suffered, threatened not, . . . neither was guile found in his mouth

–I Peter 2:21, 22, 23

O God, we thank Thee for all the brave people in the world who, though they suffer, do not complain. We are thinking of the breadwinner whose strength is failing but whose face is undiscouraged. We remember the men in office who "carry on" against personal enmities and spites which they never advertise to the public. We thank Thee for doctors, nurses, teachers, pastors who are employed in helpful ministries, undiminished in their devotion by the heavy burdens they carry in their own hearts. May Thy Holy Spirit imbue us with the same fortitude. When plans we have cherished must be abandoned, when we must carry a load of anxiety for some friend or relative who is sick or wayward or in financial distress, when we are desolate because a dear one has been taken away, help us then to be brave, to bear our part in life as usual, and to walk among our fellows in such a way that they shall never suspect the bitterness of our hearts. Give us the spirit of the uncomplaining Sufferer of Galilee. In His Name. Amen.

GOODNESS

I want to be among you to receive encouragement myself through the influence of your faith on me as of mine on you
—Romans 1:11 (New English Version)

Encourage us, O Lord, in our struggles for a better life. We thank Thee that virtue is bound to be victorious because of Thy nature. Therefore, help us to shun sin as a pest or a poison. Teach us that sin is sickness and goodness is vitality and health. Give us the joy of a conscience void of offense so that our lives may be vigorous, elastic, beautiful, and strong. So may we fill the air with health and sweetness. May we possess royal gifts of soul that shall add to the fragrance, music, aspiration, and blessing of the whole community. What a noble incentive to goodness we have, O Lord, in the possibility that our joy and strength may prove to be inspiration to others, so that the atmosphere may be filled with a wholesome purity and engaging brightness which they cannot create for themselves. Constrain us by the motive of Him who said, "For their sakes I sanctify myself." Amen.

GRIEF

Why art thou cast down, O my soul? . . . Hope thou in God —Psalm 43:5

We come to Thee, Thou Consolation of the sorrowful and Hope of the weary, because Thou alone canst comfort us. Our troubles are heavier than we can bear. Some of us are reaching out hearts and hands to Thee, empty, empty, because the lamb of our fold is with us no more. Others of us have lost a brave father or an angel mother. But we still have Thee! May we take Thy proffered hand

and keep step with Thee in acquiescence to the Divine will. Talk to us tenderly and help us to heed Thy words, so that our homes and hearts may not be so desolate. Let us no longer walk weepingly, but stoutly, bravely, and trustfully. Sustain us by the great hope of the blessed day when we shall all be together again in our eternal Home. In Jesus' Name. Amen.

GROWTH IN GRACE

Grow in the grace and knowledge of our Lord and Saviour Jesus Christ –II Peter 3:18

Lord, as we observe how the innermost character of nature is revealed in growth – how even rocks and crystals grow – rid us of complacency, of all pride in our attainments which can be but ordinary, even at their best. May we be filled with a divine discontent that shall make the wise seek to be wiser, the pure, purer, the strong, stronger. May we do every piece of work more perfectly; may we love more deeply; may we attack evil more boldly. Especially give us genuine contact with Jesus Christ. May we not be satisfied with borrowed opinions about Him or scholarly expositions of His life or eloquent sermons that laud Him, but help us to know Him and the fellowship of His cross and the power of His resurrection through the ordeal of personal and pursuing inquiry, sharp self-discipline, and brave obedience to His commands. In His light help us to see everything as it is: the true as true, the false as false. For His sake. Amen.

HE THAT OVERCOMETH

Stretching forward to the things which are before, I press on toward the goal unto the prize of the high calling of God in Christ Jesus
—Philippians 3:14

O Lord, help us not to be satisfied with average living. If there are better books to be read, may we choose them. If easygoing compliance is the way of our group, may we take the high road of the nonconformist. If our opponent stoops to a low level, may we adhere to our ideals. If others live for themselves, may we live for progress, wealth, and joy in the life of humanity. Thus may we follow in the steps of Him who, when He was reviled, reviled not again, but overcame evil with good. Lord Jesus, we put our hand in Thine. Lead us in a plain path. If Thou dost lead us uphill, walk Thou with us and the grasp of Thy conquering hand shall shame cowardice, awaken resolve, and make us strong to endure and overcome. In the Name of Him "who endured the cross, despising the shame." Amen.

HEALTH AND HAPPINESS

In thy presence is fulness of joy —Psalm 16:11

We thank Thee, Lord, that while our physical constitutions are definite, our mental state is subject to change. And we thank Thee that we can learn such self-control as to have the unruffled brows, the calm and complete and relaxed muscles which promote health. May we think, love, work, and pray as we should, and so insure a rich and even flow of life through our bodies. Save us from that worry which destroys bodily vigor, weakens the will, and condemns us to futility. Teach us the one great secret of health and happiness: to live in the presence of the best, and especially to stay close to Him who is the source of all life and who imparts His divine excellence and saving health to all who abide in Him, Jesus Christ, our Lord. Amen.

THE HIGHEST HONOR

How can ye believe, who receive glory one of another, and the glory that cometh from the only God ye seek not? —John 5:44

O Thou, who wast rich, yet for our sakes didst become poor, who wast equal with God but didst make Thyself of no reputation and didst take the role of a Galilean peasant, may we sit at Thy feet and catch Thy conception of earthly honor. Forgive our restless coveting of the praise of our fellows. Show us how we can never be our best selves if our whole aim and object in life be to receive honor from men. May we possess the freedom which is the lot of those only who are not trying to please one group today, another group tomorrow, and changing their standpoints at every turn. Make us independent, free, and strong because we have set the Lord always before us and are thinking of His rule, His approval, and His love. Give us a complacency above the assurance of kings because we have tried "to do justly, to love mercy, and to walk humbly with our God." If we may stand in Thy presence with a clear conscience, teach us how much more to be desired is simple goodness in the sight of God than earthly honor in the sight of men. In Jesus' Name. Amen.

INCREASE OUR FAITH

Surely his salvation is nigh them that fear him,
That glory may dwell in our land. . . .
Yea, Jehovah will give that which is good;
And our land shall yield its increase

—Psalm 85:9, 12

O God, our eternal Father, there are trials so sore which come to us, there are bodily sufferings so intense and prolonged, agonies of doubt so torturing, and bereavement so crushing that there is no one anywhere who can support us but Thou. All of us who are in trouble or sin turn to Thee today. Lord, increase our faith. May we not falter in a conviction of Thy goodness because of our ignorance, negligence, or the infirmity of the flesh. Deliver us from the restlessness and emptiness of a doubtful mind – "What time I am afraid I will put my trust in Thee." Grant even to the most despairing of us the fortitude and cheerfulness of a godly hope. May we lean on Thy promises – yea, give us that confidence which shall constrain us to lean on the Everlasting Arms. In the Name of Thy Son. Amen.

JUST FOR TODAY

They . . . made it a day of feasting and gladness

—Esther 9:17

O Lord God, as Thou hast watched over us and given us many blessings, help us to dedicate time and talents unto Thee. May we be happy, remembering Jesus' comforting word, "Be of good cheer, I have overcome the world." May we be satisfied, "content with such things as we have." May we fulfill our good intentions in the spirit of Dorcas "who was full of good works which she did." May we be angry, yet sin not. May we do our best with what we are and where we are. May we be imbued with a love that "beareth all things, believeth all things, hopeth all things, endureth all things." "O Lord, support us all the day long of this troublous life, until the shadows lengthen and the evening comes, and the busy world is hushed, and the fever of life is over, and our work is done. Then of Thy mercy grant us a safe lodging, and a holy rest, and peace at the last; through Jesus Christ our Lord." Amen.

KNOW THYSELF

I applied my heart to know wisdom and to know madness and folly —Ecclesiastes 1:17

Keep us, O Lord, from being bewitched by money or pleasure instead of attending to the important business of keeping our own hearts, knowing that therefrom are the issues of life and death. Save us from drifting and procrastination and help us to look into our lives to discern our mixed motives and mistakes, our possibilities and our perils. May we fearlessly measure the breadth and height of our souls no matter what the results may be. May self-surveys lead to self-conquests, self-dedications and self-improvements. May we never so neglect our most priceless inward possession that men shall look at us askance and exclaim, "What shall it profit a man if he gain the whole world and lose his own soul?" May we be true to ourselves as the first step in our loyalty to others and our adoration of Thee. In Jesus Name. Amen.

LOVE NEVER FAILETH

But now abideth faith, hope, love, these three; and the greatest of these is love

I Corinthians 13:13

We are assured, O Lord, that Christianity has revealed to us in Thee the only true and living God, because it has shown that the first and final word about Thee is love; and there is something within us that cries out with gladness to know that love is the central reality of the universe. We thank Thee that "Jesus, having loved his own which were in the world, loved them unto the end," even unto the death of the cross. We thank Thee that the early Church was so tenderly affectioned one toward another and toward Thee. All of us, O Lord, desire more sweetness in our nature. Whatever else we have, we know we have missed life's chief good if we are indifferent toward Thee or toward others. May we feel that "life is just one chance of learning love." Lord Jesus, Master of Love, teach us Thy holy art. Amen.

MAKE HASTE SLOWLY

He that believeth shall not be in haste

—Isaiah 28:16

Lord of peace, who bade Galilee be calm, speak to us and stay the headlong, muddied current of our lives. Let the waters slacken and clear and may there be more sacred emotions in the old channels because "still waters run deep." Restrain restless youth from being over-eager to meet the tasks of life. May they remember the Carpenter mending plows and harrows until He was thirty years of age. Save us from impatience because of the slow rate of our progress in attaining the likeness of Christ. May we remember that it is "first the blade, then the ear, and then the full corn in the ear." Give our characters that lasting firmness and beauty which come from "putting our work twenty times upon the anvil." Keep us trustful and devout even in the long delays of Thy providence, conscious that "they also serve, who only stand and wait." In the Name of our long-suffering Redeemer. Amen.

MINOR MORALITIES

For who hath despised the day of small things?
—Zechariah 4:10

Lord of all, as we are finding in the tiniest unit of matter a veritable universe beating with life, make us more profoundly appreciative of the values in moral behavior that we may have ignored because they seemed of trifling importance. May the parable of the small acorn and the oak teach us that any minor morality may become a major one. So help us, O God, to regard more highly and seek more carefully promptness, politeness, and patience. Help us also to cultivate cleanliness, hospitality, and moderation. Deliver us from fear, fretting, and foreboding. As Jesus valued the two mites, the sparrow fallen on the ground, the lilies of the field, and the little children, so may we realize the worth of every word, the preciousness of every act, and the undying influence of every deed. May we be given a spirit of reverence which shall control expressions, both major and minor, of our lives and bring us into harmony with Him in whom no speck or flaw was found. In Jesus' Name. Amen.

MONEY

Seek ye first his kingdom, and his righteousness; and all these things shall be added unto you
—Matthew 6:33

We thank Thee, our wise Teacher, that we are warned in Thy Word about money and told that the love of it is a root of many kinds of evil. As we endeavor not to crush but to utilize, within bounds, our natural instinct to acquire, help us both to be diligent in business and to "do unto others as we would that they should do unto us." Bless all men and women trying to make an honest living, support their families, and do their part in the general uplift of society. Bless those whose business operations are on such a scale as to involve not only their own welfare but also that of thousands of others. Give us financial leaders who are men of enterprise, initiative, and adventure, and balance them with others who are fair, just, and wise. In Jesus' Name. Amen.

NATURE AND NATURE'S GOD

And God said, Let us make man in our image, after our likeness —Genesis 1:26

Father of all Thy creatures, we desire to have a higher conception of the world of nature and humanity. These heavens bending over us at night with a thousand twinkling lights are so quietly friendly that we would not miss the message they breathe. These varicolored clouds of sunset wonder, these mountain majesties, these tasseling cornfields, these mirroring waters, these daisy-dotted meadows – surely they are expressions of the Divine. "Day unto day uttereth speech, and night unto night showeth knowledge." And if Thou dost give heavenly tongues to grasses of the fields, surely men, whom Thou hast made, are full of Thy speech. "Spirit with spirit can meet." Through the nobler gates of some of Thy sons and daughters Thou art pouring fuller tides of Thy intelligence and power and love than through others – but teach us that the smallest child is a Divine word and the most despised man is a whole message of Thine. May we honor Thy word in others and in ourselves, and behold it fulfilled in the Word which became flesh, even Jesus Christ, our Lord. In His Name. Amen.

NEIGHBORS TO HEAVEN

The invisible things of him . . . are clearly seen, being perceived through the things that are made –Romans 1:20

O God, "who dwellest in light unapproachable and full of glory," if our eyes were opened like the eyes of the servant of Elijah, we should find ourselves surrounded with golden light and set in the midst of the mysteries of eternity. Only the thin veil of sense hangs between us and the infinite. And yet the invisible things of God may be glimpsed if we will have it so by the tokens which surround us all. The far-stretching plain or woodland, the heavenly arch of blue, the love of friends, the spur of conscience, the imperatives of goodness, the vision of the pure – oh, we thank Thee for these reminders of Thee! May we climb the ladders let down for us to outlooks of appealing and eternal truth. May every ascent of faith be succeeded by a descent to the place of need, and may every experience of human helpfulness be followed again by an ascent to the mount for praise and communion and renewal of strength. In Jesus' Name. Amen.

NONCONFORMISTS

If ye love them that love you, . . . what do ye more than others? —Matthew 5:46, 47

Lord Jesus, Thy Saviourhood was the saviourhood not of one who chose the path of least resistance, who conformed to the thinking of his time and who accepted the maxims of the worldly wise, but of One who fared forth along a thorny path, and who followed His divine gleam though kinsmen and neighbors mocked, though the church rejected, and though the government sentenced to death. Thou didst not bow as we so often do to the majority. We confess, O Lord, that we have too often been conformed to this world, too often been content with ordinary public practice and average thinking. We are grateful that the scheme of things in which we are caught compels a certain average of morality up to which all must come; but may we not be satisfied with the commonplace just because we are in this social frame. In some of Thy followers, at least, we pray Thee to inspire an upward thrust that shall lift them above the business average, above the social, the educational, and the religious average, until men behold in them the superior standards and the exceptional courage which Thou didst display from Nazareth to Golgotha. In Thy Name. Amen.

OBEDIENCE AND TRUST

My times are in Thy hand —Psalm 31:15

O Lord of life and God of our salvation, it is not hints of Thee, but Thou Thyself whom we seek to know. We would get beyond the lilies and sunsets, and actually walk with Thee "in the cool of the day" We want to strike hands with the Eternal in a vital fellowship wherein we can say,

"I will trust and not be afraid" "O satisfy us early with thy mercy". Answer this major hunger of our hearts. Search us, O God, and know our hearts: try us, and know our thoughts; and see if there be any wicked way in us, and lead us in the way everlasting. May none of us make the fatal mistake of living in known sin and yet of praying to Thee, lest our prayers prove an abomination. Let us put obedience to Thee first, and then leave to Thee the direction of our lives, the destiny of our souls, and the revelation of Thyself in our experience. In Jesus' Name. Amen.

OLD AGE

Though I walk through the valley of the shadow of death,
I will fear no evil; for thou art with me.

—Psalm 23:4

O Lord, hear the prayer of those of us who are three score years and ten, and perchance four score years, and whose strength is becoming labor and sorrow. Help us to think, to repent, to believe, to hope. May we not foolishly rely upon the empty dream that death will of itself deliver us from the bonds of unrepented sin or that the soul passing from the body must inevitably come into union with God. May we recall the solemn but tender admonition, "Now is the day of salvation" and not presume upon any extension of opportunity that has not been assured us. May we rather put all our trust in Thee that we may not tremble before the mystery of the unknown world. May we be strong in the confidence that if we have union with Thee now, we shall have it hereafter. Sustain, soothe, and calm our troubled spirits until we are "like one who wraps the drapery of his couch about him and lies down to pleasant dreams," and may we say with thy servant of old, "I will trust, and not be afraid." Amen.

THE OLD, OLD STORY

The poor have good tidings preached to them
—Matthew 11:5

When other lights are failing, our heavenly Father, there is one lustrous star, the Morning Star of Righteousness, which shines on in the night. How could we part with the story of Him who once lay in a manger, ineffable beauty, sweetness, and light from heaven, who worked at a common task for thirty years, who received the world's rude buffetings, but who did not strike back or complain, who loved the young man that inquired of Him the way, "loved Martha and her sister and Lazarus," "loved his own which were in the world unto the end," who taught and prayed, who ministered and suffered as no one before or since has ever done, who was slain by those who hated him and carried to His grave by those who loved Him and was raised from the tomb by Thine Almighty hand and ever fulfills to each of us the gracious promise of His perpetual presence, "Lo! I am with you always." Lord Jesus, may no interest, care, or attraction in life keep us from Thee. Amen.

OPPORTUNITY

Behold, now is the acceptable time; behold now is the day of salvation —II Corinthians 6:2

Who is a God like unto Thee, O Lord? "Day unto day uttereth speech, and night unto night showeth knowledge." Thou art ever speaking unto us in the flowers and stars and in the upturned face of a little child. Thy voice is heard in our souls and Thy heart is seen in the face of Jesus Christ. Help us to turn the common dust of each day's experience to gold. As "now is the accepted time, and now is the day of salvation," may future years not be bound in shallows and in miseries because we have failed to remember our Creator now in the days of our youth. Remind us all when Spring is at the full, the seed must be sown. May we never need to voice the remorseful lament, "The harvest is past, the summer is ended, and we are not saved," but rather, if we have not yet made our peace with Thee, may we be given grace to say, "I will arise, and go unto my Father." In Jesus' Name. Amen.

OTHERS

The crooked shall become straight,
And the rough ways smooth;
And all flesh shall see the salvation of God
—Luke 3:5, 6

O God most merciful, who lovest all Thy children, may we heed the injunction of the Scriptures to "look not every man on his own things, but every man also on the things of others." We would pray, not for ourselves, great though our need be, but for those whose need of Thee is greater even than our own; — the destitute, the lonely, the sad, the innocent sufferers, the prisoners, the discouraged and unhappy people, the disappointed, the victims of an evil conscience, and all classes of struggling or needy people. Though tired, may they be true. Though perplexed, may they persevere. Though strained, may they be made strong in the grace which is in Christ Jesus. We ask in His Name. Amen.

OUR BOYS

I was a son unto my father,
Tender and only beloved in the sight of my mother —Proverbs 4:3

Help us who are parents of sons to realize how godlike it is to be fathers and mothers. Thou art the perfect Parent. Thou dost neither slumber nor sleep; so watchful is Thy love. Thou dost not hesitate to discipline though a sword at the same time pierce Thine own heart. Thou dost attend to us in person and not relegate us to angels, however wise they might be. O God, we want to be like Thy parental pattern. These boys are more to us than life itself. Impress upon us that we must live clean, kindly, and gracious lives for their sakes. Show us that the way of parental sacrifice is the only way by which we can hope to bring our boys to honorable manhood. We cannot pay someone else to do our part. We cannot depend upon a system outside the home. May love be the first reality of our homes and take the chief place in their lives. As these lads of ours are innocent and humble and pure to-day, we beseech Thee, Holy Spirit of God, so to guide and bless them as they ascend to manhood that by and by they shall be marked by a grown-up integrity, a grown-up humility, and a grown-up purity. We ask in Jesus' Name. Amen.

†

OUR BROTHER'S KEEPER

None of us liveth to himself, and none dieth to himself —Romans 14:7

O Lord, remind us of the subtle ties that connect us with our fellows, and of the invisible paths along which waves from our personality speed toward theirs. If we knew that, like radio, those waves proceed in every direction and without limit, how carefully should we guard our thoughts, and how faithfully should we trim our wicks so as to cast a steady and helpful light instead of a baleful and perilous gloom! Help us wherein we fail. Teach us that when a man falls, he makes it easier for some other man to fall. May we remember that our dishonesty, our impurity, our hatred, our pride are betrayals of some comrade and weaken his resolve. May we remember our Master, who knew this great social law and said, "For their sakes, I sanctify myself." May such noble unselfishness deter us, even though evil surges within. In Jesus' Name. Amen.

†

OUR GIRLS

When . . . our daughters [*shall be*] *as corner-stones hewn after the fashion of a palace. . . Happy is the people that is in such a case*
—Psalm 144:12, 15

We are grateful, O Lord, that Jesus Christ lived in a home with brothers and sisters, traveled in His public ministry not only with His disciples but also with a company of women who "ministered unto him," taught the Samaritan harlot, forgave Mary Magdalene, and loved Mary and Martha as well as Lazarus. We would commend to His sacred and all-powerful chivalry the precious girlhood of America. Increase the number of young women whose desires rise above excessive amusements and striking toilets and whose lives are marked by wise choices, refined and ennobled, that the young women of the nation shall be full of wholesome mirth, of sweetness and charm, and yet serious and purposeful in cultivating whatsoever things are lovely and true and pure and of good report. Help us to insure the dominance in American life of virtue, justice, good-will, and faith by the character of the

the women we are presenting to the coming generation. In the Name of Him who was born of the Virgin Mary. Amen.

OUR SURE REFUGE

Whom have I in heaven but thee?
And there is none upon earth that I desire besides thee —Psalm 73:25

O Father of lights and Fountain of all knowledge, grace, and power, help us to turn to Thee in every emergency of our lives as the only One who can save us in our distresses. Our friends truly sympathize with us, but no one knows us through and through as Thou dost. They try to help us, but there is no touch that really and finally heals but Thine. Music, books, work, all are helps, but O Lord, our hearts cry out for Thee, and our souls are restless till they find their rest in Thee. May we turn from sin, not merely because its wages are the death of all that is best in us, but because our iniquities always remove us farther from Thee, while "the pure in heart shall see God." In Nis Name. Amen.

PARADISE

In my Father's house are many mansions; if it were not so, I would have told you; for I go to prepare a place for you —John 14:2

O God, we thank Thee for the Father's house and the many mansions. We praise Thee for the better land toward which, as pilgrims, we are marching. We bless Thee that in that Holy City the homely language of earth shall become eloquence, for the very tongue of the dumb shall sing; and deformity below shall become beauty above, for the lame man shall leap as a hart, and the one-talent man shall go on toward a Beethoven or a Raphael or a Gladstone. We thank Thee that over there music will never be marred by a discord, or plenty mocked by fear, that happiness shall not be defeated by pain or death, but "sorrow and sighing shall flee away." O heavenly Father, give us the gladness of hope. Give us the eyes of faith to see the King in His beauty and the Holy City in its glory. And may the Saviour's words fall upon our ears, as a quieting strain of music, "Let not your heart be troubled." In the Name of our Risen Lord. Amen.

PATIENCE

Let us run with patience the race that is set before us —Hebrews 12:1

Forgive us, O Lord, if we are impatient with the weak and wavering, if we cannot bear with the dullness and indifference of average humanity, if we rebel at the slow rate of the Kingdom's advance. Give us the calmness of Jesus who waited for thirty years to begin His work. Remind us of Thy patience preparing a habitation for man throughout unimaginable ages, and leading the race forward into the light of modern civilization. With Thee a thousand years are but as a day. Show us that there is something so substantial about spiritual manhood and womanhood that its growth must of necessity be slow. May we admire patience not as the weak virtue of the passive, but as the trait of strong men and women. Give us the patience that suffereth long and is kind, that hopeth, believeth, endureth all things in the fortitude and hope of a dauntless purpose to realize the will of God in our lives and in society. In Jesus' Name. Amen.

THE PEACE OF SUNDAY MORNING

Then shall the land enjoy its sabbaths
—Leviticus 26:34

We thank Thee, O Lord, that when the Sabbath, "white with the religions of unknown thousands of years," dawns as a hallowed hour out of the deep, a holy silence, a great beneficent calm seems to rest upon the earth. It is the "peace of God which passeth all understanding." May we make good use of this weekly overture of the Divine. May we keep Sunday mornings for the great things of the soul. May they have a message for us concerning the continuing religious experience of past generations. How many such days of rest have come and gone in the fading millenniums! How many men and women, fallible and weak as we, longing and aspiring, too, as we, have thought their long, long thoughts in the sweet hush of the early hours. Ah, Lord, as we think of the unbroken succession of holy days, stretching like a great moonlit way far across the waters of the vast deep, there is a new faith and love in our hearts and we would merge ourselves with the fellowship of earth's purest and best in the Sabbath mornings of the race. Amen.

THE PERFECT MAN

Ye therefore shall be perfect, as your heavenly Father is perfect —Matthew 5:48

With all our getting, O Lord, help us to get understanding, for wisdom is the principal thing. May we grow in the knowledge of our Lord and Saviour Jesus Christ, and have such a personal grasp of His teachings that we can apply their meanings to all the major and minor situations which confront us. Though we understand all mysteries, but have not love, give us the love for others that does not spend itself in sentiment but which accepts the cross, the love which is not prompted by self-interest, but which serves with no thought of return. Thus, may our motives be honest, and may we love the approval of God more than the praise of men. Give us, then, a supreme confidence in Thee, that Thou art dealing fairly, kindly, and even lavishly, with each one of us. May we realize that we cannot do Thy will without achieving a closer walk with Thee. In Jesus' Name. Amen.

PIONEERS IN SPACE

Jehovah by wisdom founded the earth.
By understanding he established the heavens
—Proverbs 3:19

We bless Thee, O God, that truth is an eternal unity and that all creation is one united body. Be pleased to bless our astronomers, physicists, and other scientists, who have come to the aid of religion and are trying to plumb infinity. We would especially pray that in any space achievements new worlds may display new facets of Thy ever greatening glory in the heavens. Perhaps invisible potencies and influences may be transmitted from other worlds to us at whose existence we have scarcely guessed and whose values we have never known. We recall the language of the Master, "Thou hearest the sound thereof, but canst not tell whence it cometh, or whither it goeth." Hast Thou in store for Thy children great secrets from the skies? Make us diligent and reverent until we shall fare further in the compassing of Thy baffling greatness and glory. In the Name of Him through whom the worlds were made. Amen.

THE PLAYERS' PRAYER

Bodily exercise is profitable —I Timothy 4:8

Thou hast bidden us, O Lord, to rejoice in our youth and hast reminded us of the zest of the strong man who rejoiceth to run a race. We seek Thy Divine help that we may glorify Thee in our bodies and our spirits which are Thine. Like the young man of Tarsus, help us to keep our bodies under, resisting any appetites that impair quick thinking, accuracy, strength, and speed. May our passion for the game deliver us from base habits. Keep us from untempered desire to win. Help us to love fairness more than glory. May team play teach us how to live together and work together in the coming years. May we learn how to meet problems as they arise in the intricate, incessant interplay of life. Help us to be right with ourselves, our fellows, and Thee, and then to play a clean hard game, rejoicing in the tests of skill and strength and reaping the values of self-confidence, discipline, and health. In Jesus' Name. Amen.

POVERTY

The reward of humility and the fear of Jehovah
Is riches, and honor, and life

—Proverbs 22:4

Great Captain of our salvation, help us to endure hardness as good soldiers of Thine. If it is ours to be poor, may we not fret or complain, envy or covet. Help us to recognize the chance we have to play the man and become "more than conquerors," not only in all the common ills of life, but with the added tests of poverty. O Lord, perhaps we can thank Thee for poverty. As we look around us we do not always behold wheat, oil, and gold being transmuted into the "bread of life," the "oil of gladness," or the "unsearchable riches of Jesus Christ." Too often money destroys ambition, tempts the flesh, separates friends, and makes men forget God. But when we are poor, we know who are our real friends. We thank Thee for this comfort. We also have fellowship with "the Friend that sticketh closer than a brother," who cares nothing about men's bank accounts. We have leisure from life's heavy cares which many rich do not enjoy; and there is time to think, to love, and to worship. Help us Lord "in whatsoever state we are, therewith to be content." In the Name of Him "who had not where to lay His head." Amen.

✝

POWER

The gospel . . . is the power of God unto salvation —Romans 1:16

O Lord, we are thankful for the teaching of Thy Word that out of weakness we may be made strong; and we are grateful that our experience has found the promise true. Thou givest aim and direction to lives that have been feeble and uncertain. Thou dost bring up from the depths of our nature powerful emotions to take the place of the flotsam and jetsam of commonplace thinking. Thou dost reconcile flesh and spirit and other warring powers of our being and unite our hearts in Thy love and in human service. Thou dost impart the gallantry and courage of the knight so that we may exclaim with David, "By my God I will run upon a troop; by my God I will leap over a wall."

Why, then, should we do ourselves this wrong,
Or others, that we are not always strong,
That we should ever weak or anxious be,
When with us is prayer, and joy and strength
And courage are with Thee?
Amen.

PRINCIPLES

Thou therefore, my child, be strengthened in the grace that is in Christ Jesus

—II Timothy 2:1

Show us, O Lord, that every life comes to the place where the way is treacherous, where the road parts, and the more alluring path is the path of actual destruction. Remind us of life's sure surprises and its sudden tests. May we be ready. Furnish us with the principles by which we shall be infallibly guided in the critical hour. May there be something fixed in our souls, so gloriously fixed, that we cannot be easily shaken. May we be furnished with great dominating motives that shall hold us as true to Thee as gravity ties us to the sun. Let us not engage in doubtful practices, in blind following of a strong personality, or in postponing the day of strong living. Help us to live now, knowing that today conditions tomorrow and "the day of small things" is given to prepare for the Great Day which comes to try the souls of all. In the Name of Him who prepared for thirty years to serve for three. Amen.

PROTECTION

I, Jehovah thy God, will hold thy right hand, saying unto thee, Fear not; I will help thee

—Isaiah 41:13

O God, the Protector of all who trust in Thee, we are grateful for Thy watchful care over all mankind. Thou art "the keeper of Israel." Even when we forget Thee, Thou dost remember us. We therefore ask Thee, heavenly Father, to defend us in soul and body from all harm. Protect our land. Save our executives, our lawmakers, and our judges from any course that is unwise or wrong.

Guard the Church of Jesus Christ and the homes it has sanctified. Be a defense by night against the lurking powers of evil and crime. May we never fail or fall because of the temptations incident to the needful business or recreations of life. Make us strong against the mood of despair when trials and pains come upon us. Among manifold changes of life, may our hearts be fixed, trusting in the Lord, the Rock of Ages. Amen.

RELIGION BEYOND THE PALE

The good Jehovah pardon every one that setteth his heart to seek God, . . . though he be not cleansed according to the purification of the sanctuary —II Chronicles 30:18, 19

Our Heavenly Father, we are taught in Thy Word that in every nation those that sincerely seek the truth and endeavor to do right receive Thy divine encouragement. We bless Thee that there is a great host whom no man can number whose names may not be on the roll of any church but who are honestly seeking "to do justly, to love mercy, and to walk humbly with their God." Wherever there is a man "who hath clean hands and a pure heart, who hath not lifted up his soul unto vanity, nor sworn deceitfully, Lord, bless and reward that man. Show him the way of life. Guide his steps in the paths of peace. Especially lead him to know his best Friend, his divine Helper, our Lord Jesus Christ. May He become as clear as the sun, as evident as the day; and in His light may all earth's pilgrims walk till traveling days are over and all who love Thee are gathered in the Father's House at last. In Jesus' Name. Amen.

RELIGION IS SECOND NATURE

He made of one every nation of men . . . that they should seek God, if haply they might feel after him and find him —Acts 17:26, 27

Almighty God, although in perverse moments we break away from Thee to follow the devices of our own hearts, yet we know that to live apart from Thee is impossible. We tend toward Thee as surely as an arrow to its mark, as dew toward the sun, as a babe to its mother's breast. Thou hast set Eternity in our hearts. We are conscious of gnawing and confusion and want without Thy presence. There is something at work within us and beyond us inclining us to Thee. Thou hast made the world around us and the heart within to remind us of the Divine. The purple mountains, the mighty sea, the flower-tinted meadows, the love of dear ones, the spur of conscience, the quest for reality help us to recognize our unsatisfied hunger for Thee as an endowment above the price of rubies. May Thy Holy Spirit enable us to "taste and see that the Lord is good." In the Name of Jesus Christ. Amen.

REPENTANCE

There shall be joy in heaven over one sinner that repenteth, more than over ninety and nine righteous persons, who need no repentance

—Luke 15:7

Teach us, O God, that "our wills are ours to make them Thine." There are so many of us, as Thou knowest, whose wills are set in opposition to Thee. Thou hast right to the chief place in our personal life and in all our social and business relationships. We know in our best moments that the Psalmist who cried, "I have set the Lord always before me" had found the true way of living. Through Thy Holy Spirit convict us of the materialism of our thinking, the evil passions and sordid motives that rule us. Storm by the insurgence of Thy Spirit the citadel of our personality, until we abandon ourselves to the great truth which is expressed by God in Christ, with all the consequences for experience and conduct which that truth implies. Thus confer upon us the grace of sincere repentance. In Jesus' Name. Amen.

RESPONSIVENESS TO THE UNSEEN

Today if ye shall hear his voice, harden not your hearts —Hebrews 3:7

O Lord, why are we so keen for things that are low, trivial, and passing, and so dull toward Thy surpassing beauty, Thy perfect love, and Thy eternal life? Thou art our best Friend. Thou dost contend with death. Thou art the Foe of night and hate of war. Thou art the Creator of morning and the Causer of pleasure. Thou art more ready to give good gifts than we are to ask for them. Great Heart of God, we lie like helpless babes upon Thy bosom. Thou dost enfold all Thy creatures in arms that never weary. Yet, in spite of Thy nearness, we turn to the beggarly elements of the world. Made for the King's castle on the crag, we yet linger among the peasants of the plain. We are all ears and eyes for the cheap or even unwholesome, but we are inert and inanimate in the presence of shining spiritualities. But, O blessed God, Thou dost not leave us when we leave Thee. Give us grace to turn from foolish things to the eternal worth of Thy peace, Thy truth and Thy love. In Jesus' Name. Amen.

SALVATION

Know ye that the Lord he is God: it is he that hath made us, and not we ourselves; we are his people, and the sheep of his pasture

—Psalm 100:3.

O God most merciful, who dost guide the meek in judgment, who dost heal those that are broken in heart and turn the sorrow of the stricken into peace, we thank Thee for a love that is no respecter of persons. We thank Thee for the Saviour's gracious encouragement to the obscure and His tender forgiveness of the fallen. He considers our frame and remembers that we are dust. We thank Thee that our Redeemer bore our sins with His own body on the cross. And thus, O Lord, however small and insignificant we feel in the eyes of men, however ashamed because of false choices, selfish living, or fitful purposes, give us the courage still to say, "I am poor and needy, yet the Lord thinketh on me." In that royal assurance imbue us with new hope, and remember us in loving-kindness till we are carried Home in the arms of the Shepherd like "the lost sheep." In Jesus' Name. Amen.

SELF-SURVEYS

I applied my heart to know wisdom, and to know madness and folly —Ecclesiastes 1:17

Keep us, O Lord, from being bewitched by money or pleasure instead of attending to the important business of keeping our own hearts, knowing that therefrom are the issues of life and death. Save us from drifting and procrastination and help us to look into our lives to discern our mixed motives and mistakes, our possibilities and our perils. May we fearlessly measure the breadth and height of our souls no matter what the results may be. May self-surveys lead to self-conquest, self-dedication, and self-improvement. May we never so neglect our most priceless inward possession that men shall look at us askance and exclaim, "What shall it profit a man if he gain the whole world and lose his own soul?" May we be true to ourselves as the first step in our loyalty to others and our adoration of Thee. In Jesus' Name. Amen.

SHEEP OR GOATS

And he shall set the sheep on his right hand, but the goats on the left —Matthew 25:33

Search us, O Lord, and try our hearts, and show us, through Thy Holy Spirit's action, whether the dominant intention of our lives be right or wrong. May we measure ourselves by the standard set up by Jesus in His parable of the judgment. May we ask ourselves, Are we helping anybody? And if so, Is it an occasional philanthropy by which we hope to still some inward protests concerning our way of living? Is our giving a charitable sop thrown to the unfortunate, while the whole set of our hearts is selfish and perhaps wrong? Oh, teach us that better than all lip service it is to have an abiding impulse of helpfulness running through all our dreams and deeds. May we realize the mystical fact that Jesus is one with every lonely child, one with every man behind the bars, one with every pauper, one with every man hurt by injustice, one with every sufferer on a hospital bed — and may we try to serve them and thus hope to love Him. In His Name. Amen.

THE SICK

I was sick, and ye visited me —Matthew 25:36

O Lord God, who didst send Thy Son, Jesus Christ, to be the Healer of our souls and bodies, we commend to Thy love and care all who are sick. Whether suddenly stricken or weakened by long illness, whether near to death or strong in vital powers, be with them and comfort them "as a mother comforteth her child." May all who care for them show special tenderness toward their pain and weakness. May it be Thy will to bring them out of their distress. May Christ fulfill to them His promise to be with us all the days. Therefore in the valley of the shadow may they fear no evil. So sanctify to us all the distresses of life, that we shall be delivered from the bondage of the flesh and at last enjoy the liberty of the sons of God. In Jesus' Name. Amen.

†

SINCERITY

Now therefore fear Jehovah, and serve him in sincerity and in truth —Joshua 24:14

O Thou "Crystal Christ, good Paragon of God," help us to see how human, how simple, and unaffected Thy goodness was: forgiving an evil woman, lifting the children in Thine arms, preparing breakfast for Thy friends, curing lepers, showing disappointed fishermen how to make a catch. There was no pretense about Thy goodness. We would that all of us could be like Thee. Alas for so much honesty that is only prudence, for so much chastity that dares not be otherwise, for so many good deeds that expect a return, for so much fidelity to the truth for fear of being caught. Help us to gain that goodness which is genuine. Lure us by Thy example. Rule us by Thy Spirit. May we experience outbursts of real generosity, moral brakes that are automatic, ventures in Christian service that lead us along upper levels with the light of heaven on our path. In Jesus' Name. Amen.

SORROW

It became him . . . in bringing many sons unto glory, to make the author of their salvation perfect through sufferings –Hebrews 2:10

Some of us, O Lord, are dwelling in the shadow of a great sorrow. "All thy waves and billows have gone over us." We seek the calmness and trust of our Saviour Jesus Christ, "a man of sorrows and acquainted with grief," and yet ever finding in devotion to the Father and human helpfulness a compensating good that kept Him steady and strong. Let sorrow do its work in us, O Lord, but may it leave us calm in spirit, confirmed in faith, clarified in vision, and enriched in hope. In this bowl, let there be distilled the essence of human sympathy, on this hard frame let there be woven fine raiment for the soul, under these blows may there emerge the beaten gold of purified nature. So may we be "more than conquerors" through Him who walked so often in the vale of shadows and pain. In Jesus' Name. Amen.

THE STRAIN OF CITY LIFE

Now the God of peace, who brought again from the dead . . . our Lord Jesus, make you perfect in every good thing to do his will

–Hebrews 13:20, 21

As we recall Jesus' intense love for Jerusalem, we pray Thee, heavenly Father, to remember the cities of our land in mercy. We think with penitence of widespread civic dishonesty. We remember with shame the foulness of many neighborhoods, the misery of the poor and the unconcern of the rich. In the struggle for existence, we acknowledge the difficulty of avoiding the lust of gold. Deliver us from the natural sins of our environment. Help us to consider the poor who dwell amid ugliness and cramped quarters. Make us pitiful toward those who toil beyond their strength. Enable us all to bear the fret of care; to keep our souls pure, our hearts warm, and our faith steady even amid heavy toil of heart or hand. May we see Jesus Christ in our fellow men, and see Him also apart from, above, around, and behind us, ever watching, ever caring, and always helping us to overcome. In His Name. Amen.

SUFFERING

Whom the Lord loveth he chasteneth

—Hebrews 12:6

Help us, O God of all wisdom, to know that whatever is universal probably makes for happiness. Therefore, as we see the whole creation travailing in pain, may we have faith to believe it is in order to bring about a larger, richer and happier life. We thank Thee for the radiant ones in John's vision "which came out of great tribulation"; and if in our own experience we, too, must be "chiseled into character," may we be assured that a greater hand than that of Phidias or Michael Angelo is upon us. Give us that unfaltering trust which knows that there is nothing in poverty or pain and nothing in disappointment or death that can separate God's children from God's love. Through suffering, if it comes, may we be brought into a new experience of depending upon God. May we be delivered from self-centered purposes and trivial aims and equipped with that sympathy which is a healing salve for the wounds of others. In the Name of Him who taught us to pray, "Thy Kingdom come, thy will be done." Amen.

SUPREME LOYALTY

He that loveth father or mother more than me is not worthy of me —Matthew 10:37

O Divine Redeemer, we come to Thee confessing that we have not always been faithful to Thee. We have been false to Thy love and ideals because we wanted to be true to our friends. We were afraid of being called puritanical or unobliging and we have sacrificed sacred principles of conduct. We have been followers of our friends rather than of Thee. Forgive these disloyalties. Deliver us from the insidious temptation to compromise business honor, to neglect a duty, or to withhold a protest rather than to be mocked as a saint, or a Pharisee. Solomon built a pagan shrine to oblige a heathen wife, and may we also be warned by Herod who murdered the Baptist John to keep a vow. Give us an undivided heart, one that shall never yield to the temptation to charge the debt of conscience to the score of kind feeling, but shall give Thee, our Lord and Master, the pre-eminence in every moral decision. All praise to Thee, the "Paragon of God!" Amen.

SYMPATHY

Jesus, being moved with compassion, touched their eyes —Matthew 20:34

O Master of us all, we are thinking today of the way in which Thou didst lay Thyself alongside human experience and sympathize with men in this world, so weary and wicked. Thou didst not scold nor scorn even the sinner, though Thou didst warn him of the error of his way. Thou didst even pray for the unmerciful crucifiers, "Forgive them, for they know not what they do." From Thy example teach us that religion means more than the saving of one's own soul. Help us not only to see the poignant needs of humanity, but to feel with others in their hurt. Make us "wise as serpents, harmless as doves." Show us when to sympathize silently. Encourage us to believe in the undercurrent of union which flows from us through God to others, and in the power of prayer, which may go further than we dream. In the Name of the compassionate Christ. Amen.

TEMPERANCE

And every man that striveth in the games exerciseth self-control in all things

—I Corinthians 9:25

Deliver us, O God, from that self-love that encourages self-indulgence and the self-indulgence which makes us yield so often to our own desires that it becomes intemperance. Teach us that nothing can give us happiness but the triumph of reason and conscience within us. May we prize that freedom which makes the soul assert its royalty, and shun as a pest or a poison any tendency to an evil temper, gluttony, impurity, and drink. Help us to stand forth in the liberty wherewith Christ can make us free. Help us especially, as patriots, to be true to the best interest of our country and resist a traffic which corrupts politics, fills jails, increases taxes, lessens savings, destroys efficiency, and ruins homes. May the day soon come when America shall be transformed and transfigured before the nations because of her delivery from this curse of the ages, and may other lands grow wise through our example. In the Name of Jesus Christ. Amen.

THEY THAT MOURN

> *Our light affliction, which is for the moment, worketh for us more and more exceedingly an eternal weight of glory* —II Corinthians 4:17

O God of all comfort, help those today who are drooping under a great sorrow. Their anguish seems greater than they can bear as one loved one after another has been taken, or, perhaps only one, but that one the very sun of their lives. Years have brought no cure. Their bitterness grows. Teach them how to approach Thee in such a way that Thy healing may be found. We believe Thou canst give us "garlands for ashes, the oil of joy for mourning, the garment of praise for the spirit of heaviness." Work this miracle in the poor, dear hearts about us who are so desolate. If perchance the way of service to others is the cure suggested by the still, small voice, help them to recognize that "God's ways are higher than our ways" and, nothing doubting, start to fulfill the counsel of the Great Physician. In Jesus' Name. Amen.

THEY THAT SUFFER

For as the sufferings of Christ abound unto us, even so our comfort also aboundeth through Christ – II Corinthians 1:5

What a comfort, O Lord, it is for us to feel that there is a majestic purpose in all the sufferings which Thou dost permit us to undergo! The pains of disease, the antagonism of foes, the shadow of death, the loss of money, the disgrace of loved ones, the pangs of mediocrity, O Lord, Thou knowest all these and how hard they are to bear. Therefore help us to march forward on the highway of holiness, knowing that the road leadeth to the Celestial City. May we remember Jesus Christ. How He kept calm and confident in the presence of persecution! How He remained sweet amid "environing bitterness!" How bravely He suffered that others might take courage and gather strength from His example! May we "know him and the fellowship of his sufferings." May we realize that He is not far from any one of us. "The Lord is at hand." With Him at our side make us "more than conquerors" over every ill. In His Name. Amen.

UNCONSCIOUS INFLUENCE

And they took knowledge of them, that they had been with Jesus –Acts 4:13

O Lord, how many of us would be more concerned about our characters if we realized that by our unconscious influence we are impressing other lives for good or ill. It is a sobering thought that what we say or do does not touch the deepest part of others' lives, but rather the atmosphere we carry with us, betokening the inner reality of our own life. Help us to stand in awe of this spiritual energy, so silent and invisible and yet so powerful. We thank Thee for the common impulse often present even in evil people, not to hurt anyone else by their outward waywardness. But may we realize that there is something subtle and magnetic emanating from us, and that its impact upon others will be either helpful or hurtful, whether we will it or not. May more of us employ this way to help society fundamentally and lastingly by the silent, powerful contagion of a thoroughly good life. In the Name of Him whose very garments conveyed healing and holy helpfulness. Amen.

UNFALTERING TRUST

I am persuaded that neither death, nor life, nor angels, nor principalities, nor things present, nor things to come, nor powers, nor height, nor depth, nor any other creature, shall be able to separate us from the love of God, which is in Christ Jesus our Lord —Romans 8:38, 39

Help us, O God, in the hour when the shadow is falling upon us to put our trust in Thee as the One whose being and perfections are infinite, full of love and compassion, abundant in grace and truth. May we recall the word of one of Thy servants, "Though he slay me, yet will I trust him." May we have that love toward God that never faileth, "that beareth all things, believeth all things, hopeth all things, and endureth all things." So, enable us to commend by our courage and faith the gospel in whose strength we live. May some of us serve Thee as much by patience in suffering as others by diligence in well-doing, for "they also serve who only stand and wait." In the Name of the great Sufferer of Nazareth. Amen.

UNUSED TALENTS

And unto one he gave five talents, to another two, to another one; to each according to his several ability –Matthew 25:15

Some of us, O Lord, need to be startled and challenged, as Moses was, by the question, "What is that in thine hand?" As the common rod he held proved to have possibilities he had never known, may we gain a new reverence for our powers. Too often, Thou knowest, we sulk in idleness because we imagine our capacities are limited when we have never put them to the test. We say, if we knew more, if we had more money, if our social environment were different, if our health were better, and our personalities more magnetic, we would do wonders for Thee, when the powers we already have, touched by Thy spirit, could accomplish greater results. Teach us that the path of present faithfulness is the only path leading to larger service in the future. May we realize that every one of us stands out from every other, distinctive in the powers God has given him. Forbid that we should ever come up to the Judgment ashamed and saying we hid our talent in a napkin because it was so small. In Jesus' Name. Amen.

UPHILL

Thou therefore, . . . suffer hardship with me, as a good soldier of Jesus Christ –II Timothy 2:1, 3

O God, make us men when we must climb uphill. If we must overcome constitutional weakness, or chronic doubt, or the irony of fate, or the opposition of the unscrupulous, or financial embarrassment, or whatever it may be, deliver us from discouragement and make us conquerors over every difficulty. We thank Thee, our Father, that Jesus has shown us the triumphant way. "He set his face stedfastly to go up to Jerusalem." He bore His own cross to Calvary. Lift us up out of melancholy. May we be "faint, yet pursuing, chastened, but not killed." If the shade of the juniper has lured us, set us on our feet again and enable us to run in the way of Thy commandments. Oh! the thrill in the heart of him who can say, "By thee I run upon a troop, and by my God do I leap over a wall!" So empower, defend, and guide us that we shall climb all ascents of peril, be able at the end to say with the apostle, "I have finished the course," and eventually reach the mansions in the skies. In Jesus' Name. Amen.

VANITY

Remove far from me vanity —Proverbs 30:8.

Show us, O Lord, how to be educated without being conceited, how to wear good clothes, live in a nice house and drive a fine car, perhaps, without losing our good sense. Deliver us from personal vanity. Inspire us with a desire for knowledge, culture, beauty, and attainment, but help us to distinguish between pride and vanity. If we have superior wisdom, if we have been well born, if we have grace of figure or beauty of countenance, may we be taught by Thy Spirit to accept any special endowment as a trust. Putting it to the sacred use of others, may its dignity thereby become more real to us and may the possiblities of its misuse be avoided. With open eyes may we make a right choice between vanities and the virtues of Him who was meek and lowly of heart. In His Name. Amen.

WORTHY FOOTBALL

Watch ye, stand fast in the faith, quit you like men, be strong – I Corinthians 16:13

Heavenly Father, help us in every game we play not only to do our utmost and to win if we can honestly do it and if it is best, but mainly to develop in body and mind, to grow stronger in character, and richer in our sense of fellowship with other men. Even in the absorbing pleasure of running, charging, passing, and tackling, may we always keep ourselves well in hand. May we learn such implicit obedience to rules, whether we like them or not, that we shall carry this principle into other activities of life. May we have a good conscience toward bodies kept clean and vigorous by disciplined living and toward the highest ends of sport, and may we go into every game relaxed and without fear or worry, knowing that, if we lose, we have fought a good fight, and, if we win, we have deserved it. In Christ's Name. Amen.